YOUTH CRICKET COACHING

HOW TO PLAY, COACH AND WIN

YOUTH CRICKET COACHING

HOW TO PLAY, COACH AND WIN

Rob Maier
and John Stern

Published in the UK in 2013 by
John Wisden & Co.
An imprint of Bloomsbury Publishing Plc
50 Bedford Square, London WC1B 3DP
www.wisden.com
www.bloomsbury.com

ISBN 978-1-4081-9252-8

A CIP catalogue record for this book is available from the British Library.

Cover photograph © Getty Images
Photographs of youth cricket coaching sessions © Graham Morris
All other photographs © Grant Pritchard
Diagrams by Greg Stevenson

Note
It is always the responsibility of the individual to assess his or her own fitness
capability before participating in any training activity. Whilst every effort has
been made to ensure the content of this book is as technically accurate as possible,
neither the author nor the publishers can accept responsibility for any injury or
loss sustained as a result of the use of this material.

This book is produced using paper that is made from wood grown in managed,
sustainable forests. It is natural, renewable and recyclable. The logging and
manufacturing processes conform to the environmental regulations of the country
of origin.

Typeset in 11 point Joanna by Saxon Graphics Ltd, Derby
Printed and bound by Zrinski, Croatia

CONTENTS

INTRODUCTION

It is November, dark outside, and memories of summer are long gone. It is your cricket club's annual general meeting and the question is put to the floor: who will run the Under 12 side this year? Since your son/daughter plays in this team you feel a certain surge of interest and club loyalty, so you put up your hand. But what next? What are the challenges you face and what are your options?

This can be a daunting prospect even for an experienced coach, and the majority of people finding themselves in this position will not have a huge amount of coaching experience. But, with the right preparation, it is a perfectly manageable task.

You might be a parent stepping up for the first time, a teacher taking on responsibility for the school team, or a coach with a few seasons under your belt, looking for new ideas to add to your coaching skills and drills. You might be coaching players aged 9 or 15, and players who have never held a bat before or who already have the cricket bug and are keen to learn more. Whatever your circumstances, this book aims to give you everything you need to ensure you and your players get the most out of your season.

There is so much enjoyment you can get from coaching. Whatever the level or ability of your players, the sight of them growing as cricketers and people is an immensely satisfying one. This is not about discovering the next Freddie Flintoff – though that would be nice, of course – but about young people learning and developing. Cricket rewards the investment of time and effort. Its unique combination of individual contests within a team environment, its varied athletic requirements, and its endlessly fascinating tactics and strategy make it a game like no other.

Most likely you are not going to be trying to teach your players how to bowl reverse swing or a doosra. Your key task is to provide a safe, positive and fun environment for young players to enjoy their cricket, improve their skills and hopefully have some success as a group on the field during the season.

This book will help you to structure practice sessions, run drills and games that help develop the full range of cricketing skills, and manage a team on match days. You can carry this book around with you and dip in and out as you need – through the winter months when you are running indoor net sessions or during the summer as you prepare for matches.

Two final points to note at this stage: throughout the text we refer to players as 'he'. This is purely in the interests of keeping the text simple and readable, but it should be understood that we are of course referring to both boys and girls. Girls' and womens' cricket has made great developments in recent years and is it encouraging to see so many girls getting the opportunity nowadays to enjoy cricket as much as their male counterparts.

This book has been written in England for consumption by a predominantly UK-based audience. While almost all the content crosses international boundaries there are some terms and pieces of advice, such as England and Wales Cricket Board (ECB) safety regulations, which are specific to the UK. If you are based outside the UK it is worth checking with your local cricket authority for their own regulations and advice on best practice.

Key for drill and game diagrams

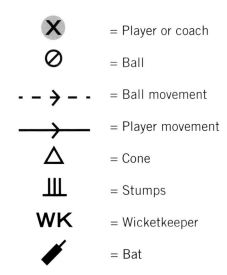

X	= Player or coach
⊘	= Ball
- - → - -	= Ball movement
——→——	= Player movement
△	= Cone
⊥⊥⊥	= Stumps
WK	= Wicketkeeper
◢	= Bat

WHAT MAKES A GOOD COACH?

1.

Anyone can be a good youth cricket coach – even without years of experience or a wall covered in coaching qualifications. A good coach will:

- communicate well with players and their parents
- motivate players to get the most out of their cricket
- provide a safe and encouraging environment in which the players can enjoy their cricket
- strike a balance between the fun and the serious

Following these basic points, any coach can provide a positive experience for their players.

FUNDAMENTAL PRINCIPLES AND PHILOSOPHIES

There are four key strands that are worth keeping in mind all the time that you are coaching your young players, remembered using the acronym F.I.S.H.

Fairness (and Fun)

Ensure that you give everyone an opportunity and do not favour one player over another. This is relevant whether you are running a net session or picking a team. Everyone will have paid for the privilege to play cricket at the club and as such they deserve the chance to play. Some players will be better than others, some will be more personable or self-confident than others (the same applies to parents as well), but you must remain as objective as possible in all areas.

Inclusiveness

Make everyone feel a bit special and important to the team. In practice sessions when you are having a discussion or a question-and-answer, do not allow one player to answer all the questions. Try to pick out players who do not speak so often, though it is vital that this is done encouragingly and with sensitivity – not everyone likes speaking up front of others. You must not make anyone feel uncomfortable.

Simplicity

It might be tempting to try to cover lots of ground during a practice session or to formulate sophisticated game plans, but it is important to focus on one or two key points. Each group of players is different and will have a different capacity to absorb information. But the best way to structure a session is to have only one or two key pieces of information that you can return to at the end of a session to check for understanding.

Honesty

Players prefer it if you are up front and honest with them. Asking open questions rather than always telling players what you think will help you engage players in the discussion and push them towards assessing their play honestly. Some examples are: 'Guys – what do you think?' 'How did that innings/bowling spell/fielding drill feel?' 'What could we have done better in that session/match/innings?' 'Remind me, what skill are we working on?' Players need to be honest with themselves, each other and about their work ethic. You will find though that younger players will respond more to instruction while the open questioning technique can be used as players mature.

Or, as the England and Wales Cricket Board's (ECB) coach education programme puts it, get SMARTER:

S – specific
M – measurable
A – achievable
R – realistic
T – time-based
E – exciting
R – reviewed/recorded

COMMUNICATING WITH PLAYERS

Communication is vital to the success of any team. You should always be willing to listen to your players and encourage an environment in which players feel able to give feedback.

How you speak to your players is also important. Avoid shouting at players or using negative language such as 'Don't bowl down the leg side' or 'Don't play across the line'; instead you can make the same point by saying 'Try to aim for that off-stump line we have discussed' or 'Look to play straight in the first few overs'. Players will stop listening if you shout or if they feel you are being overly negative. Even if players do not remember what you said or what you did, they will remember how you made them feel. Remember to be positive after a match even if they lost.

England fast-bowler Steven Finn (left) talks tactics with bowling coach David Saker.

MOTIVATING PLAYERS

Not all players will be as talented as they might like to be, but they should all be able to enjoy practice sessions and match days if you keep things interesting and give them opportunities to succeed. Introducing games and mini competitions can make practice sessions enjoyable while also aiding the learning process.

Giving players clear, achievable goals and targets can also play a key part in keeping them motivated. For example, ensure target areas for batting or bowling drills

COMMUNICATING WITH PARENTS

It is important to establish from the beginning a transparent and mutually respectful relationship with the parents of your players, of whom, of course, you may be one. It must be clear from the start what parents and players can expect from you. Many clubs enshrine these values into a charter.

A parent can expect the following from a coach:

*   A safe environment
*   Well-organised sessions
*   A positive, fair, encouraging and fun atmosphere for their children
*   The coach to be on time, to have a smart appearance and is a good role model for the children

A coach can expect the following from a parent:

*   Players arrive on time to practice sessions and matches with the right kit
*   That the values of respect for umpires, coaches, fellow parents, team-mates and opponents are reinforced
*   Ensure that player availability is communicated in a timely and unambiguous way

BEFORE YOU BEGIN

2.

FIRST CONSIDERATIONS

The first thing to realise is that the season does not begin in April. You can get to know your players and help them develop their skills in the winter nets that your club will hopefully be arranging for all its teams. This is the time when players can hone their basics or when more able players can try to develop new skills. It is also the time when you will start to see how your team might fit together and learn the personal and cricketing characteristics of your players.

Ideally you should recruit another coach or volunteer to help you out. It is a huge amount of work for one person to manage every aspect of running a squad of 15 or more young people. Not only are there plenty of logistics and administration to attend to, but running net and practice sessions on your own will be demanding. By far the best scenario is to team up with a willing ally who can share the load and with whom you can discuss ideas and plans. That way, your practice sessions will be much more fun and productive for all concerned.

The ECB guidelines suggest a coach-to-player ratio of one to eight, so it is highly desirable to have an assistant (perhaps one of your club's better players, in his late teens and keen to develop coaching skills – anyone 16 or over is eligible to take an ECB Level 1 coaching course) or an enthusiastic parent in attendance, not only to assist in the running of the activities but also in case of emergency. If you are on your own and an accident occurs you will most likely have to stop the session.

WORKING WITH A GROUP FOR THE FIRST TIME

You will want to acquire as much information as possible about the group you are going to coach. Find out, for example, how much experience they have of hard-ball cricket or whether they are used to soft balls.

Ensure that you have any relevant medical information relating to your group, such as allergies or injuries, and all the contact details of the players' parents in case of any accident.

What you will need

1. A players' information check sheet (see example below/opposite)
2. A players' attendance register
3. First aid point – plus access to emergency numbers if you need them
4. To be Criminal Records Bureau cleared
5. To have completed a Safeguarding and Protecting Children course

	First name	Surname	Parent contact	Home number	Mobile
1					
2					
3					
4					
5					
6					
7					
8					
9					
10					
11					
12					

Email	Batting RH/LH	Bowling RH/LH	Wicket-keeper	Comments	Medical information

SAFETY

Your first priority is to ensure that the coaching and playing environment is safe. Check for any holes in the nets or water on the floor. Check that the lighting is satisfactory and that the batting mats are accessible.

During coaching sessions, players' kit should ideally be left outside the sports hall so that players are not in danger of tripping over it when they are padding up.

You must always be mindful of the ECB fast-bowling directives so that young bowlers are not overloaded. More information can be found on the ECB website (www.ecb.co.uk) and also on page 119.

CLOTHING

At the start of your coaching season you should encourage players to wear club clothing for all coaching sessions and match days. If there are players in the group who have achieved higher honours and perhaps represented the county, they should not be permitted to wear county kit at club sessions. It indicates separation from the other players and can cause resentment. Tracksuits are fine, though whites are good too. You want the players looking like cricketers as it creates a good impression both within the group and also to opponents, when you are playing matches. This is all part of the aspiration to be as good as you can possibly be.

It is also absolutely vital that the coach should look the part and create a good impression. If you expect the players to be switched on and focused then the least they can expect from you is the same. Even if you have had to dash straight from work, try to make sure you have a club tracksuit or similar that you can quickly change into. Remember that you are there to lead by example.

In winter, players should be encouraged to err on the side of wearing too many layers of clothing rather than too few. Layers can always be removed but you do not want players being cold.

SETTING UP THE SESSION

Once you have all the background information you need and you have a safe and suitable environment in which to coach, it's time to start the session.

It is important to plan your practice sessions and you should have a clearly thought-out session ready to go. However, you will also need to be flexible. Things will not always turn out as you expect, as players may pick things up more quickly than you imagined or find an activity particularly demanding.

Get the players positioned within earshot so you can speak to them comfortably without having to shout. This is when you should explain to them briefly and clearly what you will be working on in the upcoming session. Keep it brief.

CONCENTRATION DURING THE SESSION

Without being dictatorial, it is important to set some clear ground rules before you start. For example, you might state that there should be no bouncing of balls, and insist on players being quiet while you are talking, particularly for important matters like safety.

It is impossible for anyone, let alone a youngster, to hit balls or run around non-stop for an hour and a half. So make sure that players have regular, short breaks when they can rehydrate. You can combine these breaks with reviews and feedback on the activity the players have just participated in. Encouraging parents to make sure their children are fed before coming to a practice session will help players to maintain focus.

Players will get tired, but the coach must try to ensure they do not become bored or distracted. Maintain that sense of fun and enjoyment and also achievement. With older players, you can lay it on the line a bit more by empowering them with the choice: do they want to hit 60 balls well or 60 balls badly? Explain to them that hard work reaps rewards, that they will see the benefit of the practice sessions when they step over the white line in the summer.

Always be mindful too of the space available versus numbers ratio and the number of nets available. The maximum number of players you would ever want to have in a net is eight; more than that and bowlers will become too easily distracted.

Coaching equipment

Hopefully your club will be able to supply a decent amount of kit. If not, encourage them strongly to do so. All the equipment listed over the page is readily accessible, and it is possible to buy coaching packs, which are a great starting point. Equipment is always changing, developing and being adapted from other sports, so while these items cover most of the bases, it is a good idea to keep abreast of innovations. Feel free to experiment with different equipment, so long as you plan properly how to use it and make sure the set-up is safe.

ESSENTIAL KIT

Balls: Have a good supply of soft balls (tennis, IncrediBalls®, plastic) and hard balls – old cricket balls are good for fielding drills as they do not sting too much.

Bats: Plastic bats are good for the junior groups as they are light and easy to handle. Please encourage all hard-ball cricketers to have their own box and helmet as these are personal items and players are reluctant to share!

Bibs: You will need these for team games and warm-ups. If bibs are not available then remind players to bring both a coloured and a white shirt for team identification.

Coloured cones and discs: For marking out various drills, games and activities, and bowlers' run-ups.

First-aid kit: An essential, and make sure it includes freeze spray for those hard-ball knocks.

Stumps: Minimum of six sets, two each for three nets. Many indoor facilities will have stumps so you may not need to purchase these.

Tape: Most indoor facilities will require the use of mats for cricket to be played. These will need to be stuck down securely, and tape can also be used to create targets for the bowlers to aim at.

Also nice to have:

Baseball catching mitt: This is very useful for coaches when running fielding drills for receiving throws with a hard ball.

Bowling machine: Very good for grooving technique, but this is expensive kit and needs to looked after and operated only by adults. The bowling machine also requires its own special balls.

Chalk: Useful when trying to discuss bowling alignment, and bowlers often use this to mark out run-ups.

Clip board: This is useful when making notes, but ensure that you get actively involved in the session as players will respond far better to this.

Andrew Flintoff puts his mitt to good use in his Lancashire days.

Crash mats: Great for diving and bowling drills. Most school gyms have these, but make sure you get permission to use them. Other fitness equipment that can be found in schools gyms is also useful, such as skipping ropes, benches and resistance equipment. Just use your imagination!

Reaction balls: When you drop these they bounce in crazy directions and it helps players stay low and work dynamically on the balls of the feet.

Reaction boards: Great for catching drills as the ball deviates once it has struck this.

Roll-up mats: The basic way of creating a consistent and safe bounce for a net session, unless you have the good fortune to be practising in a cricket-specific hall.

Equipment for fitness and movement, also known as speed, agility and quickness: This includes ladders, hurdles, cones, poles, resistance equipment (see chapter 5, 'Warm-up and fielding drills').

Pitch maps: This is a poor man's Hawk-Eye! If these are recorded honestly and as accurately as possible, they give a good indication of how consistent your bowlers are. The areas you will need to look at are: full, good and short length.

Tennis racket: Very useful for catching drills with tennis balls.

Two-tone cricket balls or IncrediBalls®: These are great for seeing how the bowlers are releasing the ball and whether they are maintaining an upright seam position, which is vital for swing bowling.

Video camera: This is a very useful and fun addition to the coaching armoury, as players can learn a lot from seeing footage of themselves playing. You must, however, make sure you get parental permission before doing this.

Wobble boards: Great for bowling and batting balance drills.

STRUCTURED COACHING PROGRAMME FOR WINTER NETS OR SUMMER SEASON

3.

THE PROGRAMME

This is a programme of twenty 90-minute coaching or practice sessions that can be used for a winter nets programme or through the summer evenings for squad practices. It is not supposed to be a rigid programme that must be adhered to, but a menu with a number of varied options for the coach to pick and choose from as he gets to know his group of players. The more you know about your players the better you can structure a session. All drills and activities are designed for maximum participation.

The programme begins with soft-ball cricket for younger or less experienced players, progressing through to an introduction to hard-ball cricket and beyond. If a coach is in charge of a relatively experienced group the programme can be picked up around session 11. But many of the basic drills and activities apply across different age groups and ability levels. Many drills can be adapted to suit more advanced players by introducing more challenging elements. Many drills are, in fact, best conducted with soft balls, for safety reasons.

Certain drills and activities will soon emerge as favourites that a coach will want to come back to time and again. It is important that players never become bored or too used to certain drills and activities. However, there is no escaping the necessity of repetition when it comes to effective practice. Ultimately, players will want to bat and bowl in the nets, but it is important that net sessions have their structure just like the more clearly defined drills and activities.

Above all, the important thing to remember is that every session must be safe and fun. If players are to keep coming back then it is vital that they enjoy themselves and leave every session with a sense of achievement. The following four points will help you pull this off:

- Get the players into an activity as soon as possible
- Explain activities clearly and concisely
- Do not overload players with information but do check them regularly for understanding
- Stick to only one or two key technical or coaching points that you want to communicate in each session, and then discuss them in a short debrief at the end of every session to ensure understanding

Each session is broken down into four elements:

- Warm-up activity
- Key session focus
- Secondary session focus
- Session debrief

The warm-up can be anything from a game of dodgeball to a fielding drill, but the important thing is that it is quick and energetic. Try to ensure that the warm-up activity is set up before the players arrive so the session can start straight away and there is minimum hanging-around time. The key session focus is typically a drill from which the key coaching points will be derived and to which the coach will return at the end of the session. The secondary session focus will typically be a skills-based game or a net session. At the end of the session it is important to bring the players together, let them calm down and revisit the key points that they learned in that session.

It is important that the coach clearly demonstrates all activities before the players undertake them themselves. If you have not played that much cricket yourself or are not too confident about certain aspects of the game then it is vital that you seek out advice or assistance from a more experienced coach or player at your club. Another option is to get hold of video footage. Players should be encouraged to observe how the best players go about playing the game. Much can be learned from seeing the top county and international players perform.

However good your cover-drive might be, watching Ian Bell play it could be the best lesson any young player has.

All the drills and activities that appear in these sessions are based around a group of approximately 12 players. **Each one is explained and illustrated in the coming chapters.** Timings are a guide only. Some activities will take longer than you imagine; others you may wish to cut short and allow more time for something else. There are no hard and fast rules other than that your players should have fun in a safe environment and develop their skills.

THE SESSIONS
Session 1
Warm-up (15 mins): Introduction and welcome followed by **fitness and movement** stations (see chapter 5, 'Warm-up and fielding drills', p31–38). **Tip:** make sure these are set up in advance of the session so the activity can begin straight away.

Key session focus (30 mins): Batting set-up (see chapter 6, 'Batting drills and games', p89).

Secondary session focus (40 mins): Pairs batting, using a soft ball: a reward for the more disciplined drill-type activity that has been the main focus of your session (see chapter 6, 'Batting drills and games', p100).

Session debrief (5 mins): This is a chance to gather your players together, for them to warm down and rehydrate, and to discuss some key points of the session such as the importance of balance and establishing a firm base. Static stretching is a good warm-down activity and a good habit for your players to get into. Ensure that your players have all their kit before they go home.

Session 2
Warm-up (10 mins): Hand hockey (see chapter 5, 'Warm-up and fielding drills', p39).

Key session focus (20 mins): Overarm throwing in pairs using soft balls (see chapter 5, 'Warm-up and fielding drills', p44–45).

Secondary session focus (60 mins): Continuous cricket (see chapter 8, 'Middle games and practices', p122).

Session debrief (5 mins):
Recap some key points such as staying side on and keeping the front arm high.

Session 3
Warm-up (10 mins): Piggy in the middle (see chapter 5, 'Warm-up and fielding drills', p38).

Key session focus (45 mins): Straight-line bowling (see chapter 7, 'Bowling drills and games', p110). Key coaching points include: head and front arm travelling down the line. Be mindful not to overload information. Always check for understanding.

Secondary session focus (30 mins): Bowling competition (see chapter 7, 'Bowling drills and games', p116).

Session debrief (5 mins): Recap key points from bowling drill PLUS ask players to bring hard-ball kit for the next session when they will receive an introduction to hard-ball cricket.

Session 4
Warm-up (20 mins): Dynamic stretching (see chapter 5, 'Warm-up and fielding drills', p31–38) (10 mins) followed by **fitness and movement** (10 mins).

Key session focus (50 mins): Introduction to hard-ball cricket with a heavy focus on **net safety** (15–20 mins) followed by a **basic net session** (30–35 mins) (see chapter 4, 'Net sessions', p26).

Secondary session focus (15 mins): Group catching competition (see chapter 5, 'Warm-up and fielding drills', p55).

Session debrief (5 mins): Recap on the importance of net safety.

Session 5
Warm-up (10 mins): Vortex (see chapter 5, 'Warm-up and fielding drills', p40).

Key session focus (25 mins): Straight-line bowling (p110). Recap the points discussed in session 3 and introduce new elements such as how to grip the ball.

Secondary session focus (50 mins): Tip and run (see chapter 8, 'Middle games and practices', p124).

Session debrief (5 mins): Discussion and reminder of key points such as how to grip the ball.

Session 6
Warm-up (10 mins): Dodgeball (see chapter 5, 'Warm-up and fielding drills', p41).

Key session focus (25 mins): Batting drill – **front-foot drive** (see chapter 6, 'Batting drills and games', p96).

Secondary session focus (50 mins): Front-foot drive game (see chapter 6, 'Batting drills and games', p99).

Session debrief (5 mins): Discuss some key points from the session: hands coming from high to low. Ensure that your players have all their kit before they go home.

Session 7
Warm-up (10 mins): Fitness and movement, p39. It might seem repetitive but it is such a good way of helping to improve young players' movement and agility.

Key session focus (25 mins): Bowling drill – **line and length** (see chapter 7, 'Bowling drills and games', p111).

Secondary session focus (50 mins): Bowling grid under pressure followed by **bowling competition** (see chapter 7, 'Bowling drills and games', p115–116).

Session debrief (5 mins): A key point from this session might be bowling a good length. Remind players to bring hard-ball kit for the next session.

Session 8
Warm-up and key session focus combined (35 mins): Team relay fielding (see chapter 5, 'Warm-up and fielding drills', p79). This is a great warm-up,

or can be extended into a warm-up plus fielding session that becomes your key session focus. With a net session to come, this will be physically tough, so ensure that frequent breaks are taken.

Secondary session focus (50 mins): Group hard-ball nets – **'out is out'**. Batsmen learn for the first time the consequences of their actions (see chapter 4, 'Net sessions', p28).

Session debrief (5 mins): Discuss how the players found the 'out is out' net session. What did they learn?

Session 9

Warm-up (10 mins): One-bounce box game (see chapter 5, 'Warm-up and fielding drills', p42).

Key session focus (25 mins): Batting – **pull shot** (see chapter 6, 'Batting drills and games', p97–98).

Secondary session focus (50 mins): Continuous cricket (see chapter 8, 'Middle games and practices', p122).

Session debrief (5 mins): Recap on a key point from the pull-shot drill such as hands coming from high to low. Remind players to bring hard-ball kit for next session.

Session 10

Warm-up (10 mins): Underarm stump aim (see chapter 5, 'Warm-up and fielding drills', p64).

Key session focus (25 mins): Spin-bowling basics (see chapter 7, 'Bowling drills and games', p112).

Secondary session focus (45 mins): Group hard-ball nets – **two batsmen per net** (see chapter 4, 'Net sessions', p29).

Session debrief (5 mins): Static stretching (p31–38) followed by a session debrief to discuss key focus points such as how to spin the ball and which direction it went in.

Session 11

(From now on it is expected that every player will come prepared for hard-ball sessions, even though many activities will still use a soft ball.)

Warm-up (10 mins): Dynamic stretching and **fitness and movement** (p31–38).

Key session focus (30 mins): Short fielding and **boundary fielding** (see chapter 5, 'Warm-up and fielding drills', p60–63). Split players into two groups if you have an assistant or a willing parent to help. The coach should ensure that the area is safe and that the two groups are throwing the ball away from each other because this is a hard-ball session. Swap groups halfway through.

Secondary session focus (45 mins): Group nets – **points for contact** (see chapter 4, 'Net sessions', p28).

Session debrief (5 mins): Discussion points include where you pick the ball up from, no gaps in long barrier.

Session 12

Warm-up (10 mins): Dodgeball (see chapter 5, 'Warm-up and fielding drills, p41).

Key session focus (50 mins): Batting – **sweep shot** followed by **sweep-shot game** (see chapter 6, 'Batting drills and games', p98 and p103).

Secondary session focus (25 mins): Target batting (see chapter 6, 'Batting drills and games', p101).

Session debrief (5 mins): Discuss the execution of the sweep shot.

Session 13

Warm-up and fielding game (30 mins): Dynamic stretching (p31–38) followed by **wall catching** (see chapter 5, 'Warm-up and fielding drills', p46).

Key session focus (25 mins): Straight-line bowling (p110). Recap previous coaching points such as head and front arm travelling down the line and grip.

Introduce discussion about how to swing the ball. Two-tone IncrediBalls® work well for this. Always check for understanding.

Secondary session focus (30 mins): Bowling competition (p116).

Session debrief (5 mins): Discussion might involve how to swing the ball. This is not something that will be learned overnight. The coach must exercise judgement about when to introduce progressions.

Session 14

Warm-up (10 mins): Fast throw and catch (see chapter 5, 'Warm-up and fielding drills', p50).

Key session focus (25 mins): Soft hands (see chapter 6, 'Batting drills and games', p102).

Secondary session focus (50 mins): Running between the wickets game (see chapter 6, 'Batting drills and games', p105).

Session debrief (5 mins): Recap on soft hands and hitting into the gaps.

Session 15

Warm-up (10 mins): Fitness and movement (p31–38).

Key session focus (25 mins): Wicketkeeping drill (see chapter 5, 'Warm-up and fielding drills', p82).

Secondary session focus (45 mins): Group nets – **two batsmen per net** (p29).

Session debrief (5 mins): Key points from the wicketkeeping drill include: hand and fingers pointing down.

Session 16

Warm-up (10 mins): Hand hockey (p39).

Key session focus (40 mins): Batting circuit – selection of 1. **Duck and swerve**, 2. **Front-foot isolation**, 3. **Head to line**, 4. **Wall work**, 5. **Bench batting**,

6. **Bean-bag balance**. Players in pairs, a few minutes per station (see chapter 6, 'Batting drills and games', p89–93).

Secondary session focus (35 mins): Tip and run (p124) (see chapter 8, 'Middle games and practices').

Session debrief (5 mins): Discuss the importance of balance. Provide players with field-settings information to read before next session.

Session 17

Warm-up (10 mins): Relay fielding (see chapter 5, 'Warm-up and fielding drills', p77).

Key session focus (40 mins): Field settings game including **fitness and movement/dynamic stretching** element (see chapter 9, 'Field settings' p135).

Secondary session focus (35 mins): Group nets – **two batsmen per net** (p29).

Session debrief (5 mins): Recap on field settings.

Session 18

Warm-up (10 mins): Fitness and movement (p31–38).

Key session focus (25 mins): Bowling. Recap previous focus points from **straight-line bowling**. Remind players of the importance of getting everything to move towards the target and ensure they complete the action. Progress to changing angles for bowling at left-handed batsmen by adjusting angle of run-up and bowling at a target (as in **line and length bowling**, p111).

Secondary session focus (50 mins): Group nets – **points for contact** (p28).

Session debrief (5 mins): Discuss key points from bowling recap. Vital to check for understanding among players.

Session 19

Warm-up (10 mins): One-bounce box game (p42).

Key session focus (25 mins): Batting drill – **pull shot** using underarm feeds (see chapter 6, 'Batting drills and games', p97–98).

Secondary session focus (50 mins): Group nets – **out is out** (p28).

Session debrief (5 mins): Discuss key points from the pull shot such as **hands coming from high to low**.

Session 20

Warm-up and fielding (15 mins): Dynamic stretching (p31–38) followed by **vortex** (p40).

Key session focus (65 mins, no secondary session focus): Player-led group nets – if this is your last practice session of the winter programme, this is a good time simply to let the players take responsibility, to instil the 'practise as you play' mantra and give the players length opportunities to bat and bowl before you begin the season.

Session debrief (10 mins): You might want to make this a little longer, to recap on some of the things the players have learned and things you hope to achieve during the coming season.

NET SESSIONS

4.

INTRODUCTION TO HARD-BALL CRICKET

The importance of a proper safety briefing when players are first introduced to hard-ball cricket cannot be overstated. It is vital that the coach is familiar with the space he is working in. Find out how much space you have available and also what sort of space it is. This will play a major part in deciding what sort of activities you can partake in. For winter sessions you need to know how many individual nets are available, what sort of floor surface the sports hall (or equivalent) has and what sort of equipment is available to use.

When it comes to summer outdoor practice a coach needs to know in advance what else might be going on at the club. Is there a match going on at the same time? Will any of the nets be in use at the same time? How much space will be available to use safely? A coach does not want to turn up with an array of intricate plans and then find that he does not have the facilities to put them into action.

If working indoors, pull out the nets and check for any safety issues such as holes or water on the floor. Roll out the batting mats and ensure that the ends are taped down so the ball will bounce safely in the nets. Find a safe area where batsmen can pad up. Ideally this might be to the side of the nets. If there is not space it might have to be outside the sports hall. They must not pad up in an area behind the bowlers where they could be hit by a ball.

Then it is time to talk about the players' own personal safety: they should never turn their backs on the batsmen when walking out of the nets; when batting, they should use their bats to retrieve a ball that is hit into the net; and they should return the ball to the bowler with an underarm throw rather than a kick or a hit back with the bat. This is a really important part of a young player's cricket education. They will carry these basic lessons in safety for the rest of their cricketing lives so it is vital to ensure that they understand what is being said.

Make sure you have a fully equipped first-aid kit, all the parents' contact numbers and an incident book. While one always hopes that no one will get hit by a cricket ball, there is no escaping the fact that it does happen. And you need to be able to deal with any incident – however small – quickly, efficiently and sympathetically.

Try to build confidence so that players are not shying away from the ball either when batting or in the field. This has very little to do with age: you will find much older players who still have issues about being afraid of the ball, which can hinder their progress. Equally, you can see younger kids who have no fear at all. It is important to try and build that confidence early on. It is vital that players watch the ball at all times.

NET SAFETY ESSENTIALS

1. A batsman must use **only his bat** to retrieve a ball if it is nestled in the net at the back or side of the stumps. He must not reach in with his hand because there is a very real danger of being hit the by the ball in an adjoining net.

2. After a bowler has received the ball back from the batsman he must return to the bowling run-up area without turning his back on the batting areas of the nets so he can avoid any ball that may be hit out in his direction.

3. Make sure that the padding-up area is safe and not anywhere where players might be hit by a ball. Ideally to the side of the nets if there is space, or if need be outside of the hall itself. What you cannot have is batsmen padding up behind the bowlers' run-ups where they are in the batsmen's line of shot. That is very dangerous.

NET SESSION OPTIONS

Basic net session (see session 4)

Anyone who has played a decent amount of cricket will know how aimless net sessions can become if they are poorly managed: batsmen bat without discipline; bowlers become bored and tired. This is when net sessions can become pointless and dangerous.

When players are being introduced to hard-ball net sessions for the first time, it is advisable simply to let them enjoy the experience of batting and bowling in a safe environment. There will be plenty of time to introduce more focused, disciplined and competitive elements to these sessions later on.

Net sessions can be a challenge to the ideal of maximum participation because not everyone can be batting and bowling at the same time. If there is enough space to the side of the nets, the waiting batsmen can play some mini-games such as keepy-uppy, where they try to keep a cricket ball in the air with their bat. Another option, depending on the ability of the group, is that the waiting batsmen give each other drop feeds to hit: six balls and then swap with their partner. This only works if you have a safe space to the side of the nets.

Hard-ball kit essentials

Helmet	Abdominal protector (box)
Gloves	Pads
Thigh pad	Bat

People do worry when it comes to hard-ball cricket that there is going to be huge expenditure. There will be certain things that need to be purchased and you do find that players are not too keen on sharing equipment such as helmets. But initially you can get by with limited outlay and many clubs will have a club kit bag with the essential items. The absolute minimum in terms of kit should be a box. In addition, each player should ideally have his own batting gloves, batting pads, thigh pad and helmet.

With bats, it is not necessary or desirable to spend vast amounts of money on a top-of-the-range bat that the player may grow out of within a year. Make sure the bat can be picked up and swung easily. The biggest mistake is for a player to have a bat that is too heavy for him. If he cannot easily lift the bat and play shots comfortably it really affects his game and, of course, his enjoyment. When choosing a bat, the player should be able to swing it freely. Ideally, bats should be purchased from a reputable cricket-specialist retailer that can offer advice on buying the right bat.

England's Jonathan Trott and Kevin Pietersen kitted out for a net session.

Out is out (see sessions 8, 19)

How it works: Players operate as for a normal net session but a batsman leaves the net when he is out. There will need to be more batsmen padded up and ready to go than would normally be the case.

Another option is to designate one of the nets a 'practice' net, so when a batsman is out he goes into the practice net and the new batsman comes into the 'live' net, where he can score runs but also be given out. There is a lot of subjective judgement here. The coach needs to give the batsman a notional field setting and give him runs scored accordingly. Likewise, if he edges a catch to the keeper or hits a catch to where a fielder was notionally set then he is out. If batsmen are out quickly then simply conduct another innings.

Coaching aims: To make batsmen understand the consequences of their actions and also to develop the mantra of 'practise as you play'.

Points for contact (see sessions 11, 18)

How it works: Because 'out is out' can be quite subjective and because good batting is not only about run-scoring, another option is to reward batsmen for good contact with the ball. The batsman gets one point for making the best possible contact on the ball, no points for moderate or poor contact, and he loses a point if he plays a loose shot or is out.

This works better for more advanced players who understand clearly what shots to play and with whom you can have a dialogue about what they are trying to achieve. Players also need to be honest for this to work well.

To make this activity more measurable, one option is to break it down into segments of, say, 10 balls each, then review and add up the batsman's score. This works for bowlers too. They score a point if they hit the right area (which can be chalked on to a net mat), zero if they just miss it, and they lose a point if the ball goes down leg or they are punished.

Coaching aims: Players focus on the process rather than the outcome, trying to execute the right shot or delivery.

Progression: Add in some cones to indicate hitting or scoring areas as a way of challenging the batsman further.

Group nets – two batsmen per net (see sessions 10, 15, 17)

How it works: Split your bowlers into certain nets. Quicker bowlers across two nets and spinners into another with a wicketkeeper. For the spinners net the stumps will have to come forward to allow space, but the bowler's stumps must be moved back accordingly. The batsman's stumps should be moved from the batting crease to the popping crease (where the batsman stands). Mark a new popping crease with chalk or cones. At the other end move the bowlers' stumps back the same distance.

Have two batsmen padded up and batting in each net. This will reduce your bowling numbers but, depending on the size of the group, will offer great opportunities to the bowlers and also help to maximise participation, which is always the goal of any session. Having six or seven bowlers in a net can be a very unsatisfactory experience, as players get distracted easily because they are not actively involved between each delivery and never develop any sort of rhythm.

Batsmen must run every third ball and call for the run as they would do in a game. It is also a chance to check on their running lines: they must run on opposite sides of the pitch to each other. Give each pair roughly 12 minutes' batting each, but swapping nets after four minutes.

The coach should always be mindful of the numbers of players involved and adjust the session accordingly. However, you must always be mindful of the ECB directives for junior fast bowlers (see page 119) and ensure that no one is overloaded.

Other options are to have a bowling machine in one net or designate it a 'drills net', where batsmen can practise a certain shot in pairs with a drop or bobble feed.

Match scenarios

How it works: This is one for more experienced players, particularly as you move towards the start of your season. Start by giving your quick bowlers brand new balls, if possible, and have them bowling at your top-order batsmen. Get the bowlers to think about the areas that they will bowl at the start of the innings: full, outside off stump, maybe trying to find the outside edge. Ask the batsmen how they are looking to play at the start of the innings: playing straight, not being loose outside off stump, using the whole face of the bat.

Have your spinners in another net bowling to middle-order batsmen. Discuss field setting options with your bowlers and have your batsmen looking to play with soft hands to accumulate those singles. Then you might look at end-of-innings scenarios and give your quick bowlers old balls and have them trying to bowl yorkers.

WARM-UP AND FIELDING DRILLS

5.

Whether you are beginning a practice session or getting ready for a match, it is important to get your players warmed up physically and mentally so that they can get the most out of the practice or match that is to come. As a coach you will inevitably do plenty of talking, but the best way to begin a session is to get your players into an activity as soon as possible. This is the most effective way to maintain their mental and physical motivation.

Watch any county or international side warming up before a match and you will see a variety of activities taking place. Not all of them will appear to be cricket-related, but they offer two key things: physical activity, and game-related drills and movements that players will use during a match. Players of all ages and abilities love to be involved in a competitive environment with their mates. For a group of players who will all be pulling together when they are in the dressing room or on the cricket field these little games are a great way to inject some light-hearted internal competition. They are guaranteed to get the blood flowing and ensure players begin a match or practice session with a positive mental attitude. The coach has to drive the enthusiasm and the passion, and to ensure that every player goes away from a session with a sense of having achieved something. This is what will make players come back and want to continue playing the game.

The fielding drills that follow also serve a purpose as a way of warming up for a session or a match. There are no hard and fast rules as to what you should do when; it is up to you to judge the needs of your group at any one time. A selection of these games and drills appear in the template for a structured season- or winter-long programme in chapter 3. This is all food for thought, tried-and-tested examples of drills and activities that work. But the coach will be the best judge of what is working and what is not. If players are finding something too easy, make the activity more challenging. Where appropriate, examples are given of how to progress or advance certain drills. The ultimate aim is for a coach to be able to think on his feet, to be confident enough to review each session, and to invite feedback from players about the sessions.

Some activities are dependent on space, and some that utilise the walls of a sports hall or indoor cricket centre are clearly designed for indoors, but most activities can be equally undertaken inside or outside, as part of winter or summer programmes. Some games and drills specify whether only a soft ball should be used, but where it is not specified a hard ball can be used if players are sufficiently experienced. Some games and drills are better for younger or less experienced players. These will tend to appear earlier in their relevant sections. Most drills are explained and illustrated based on an approximate group size of 12 players so that they can be used as match-day warm-ups or practice sessions. Some drills benefit from the presence of two coaches, or maybe just a willing parent or an enthusiastic young adult from one of your club's senior teams.

Note: Distances and measurements for the set-up of warm-up games and fielding drills are there as a guide only. Optimum measurements will depend on a number of factors such as space available and the age and ability of the players. The set-up for many of the drills involves setting out a very basic square grid the size of which has been suggested as 10m by 10m. This is only a guide. The grid can be any size of your choosing as long as the drill is safe and productive.

WARM-UP ACTIVITIES
Fitness and movement, also known as speed, agility and quickness
(see chapter 3, sessions 1, 4, 7, 11, 15, 18)
It is vital that players develop their athletic abilities as well as their cricket skills; indeed, the two go hand in hand. The fitter or more agile a player is, the better cricketer he will be.

Fitness and movement is a great warm-up for a session and there are so many ways to vary the use of equipment. It is also possible to combine fitness and movement with fielding, whereby you might have a fitness and movement station such as a ladder or hurdles that lead into a fielding station where a player has to catch or collect a ball.

Set-up and equipment: Place a cone and then five or six hurdles set out in front of you about half a metre or one pace apart. Players jump over the hurdles, round another cone at the end of the hurdle line, and return to join the back of the queue of players.

You can add a cricket element to this by having one of the players behind a stump beyond the final cone. As the player completes the hurdle, the player behind the stump rolls him the ball and he in turn rolls it at the stump. The runner goes to the stump and the player at the stump goes to join the back of the queue waiting to complete the hurdles.

The basic fitness and movement equipment includes small hurdles, ladders, cones and poles.

Kevin Pietersen practises his hurdling.

Graeme Swann moves sideways through a set of small hurdles.

Additional equipment includes parachutes and resistance belts, where a team-mate tries to hold a player back as he runs.

England train with resistance belts.

As an example, set up four stations with the players split up into four groups. Players spend 2–3 minutes on each station.

Coaching aims: Some key points to look out for include encouraging players to stay on the balls of their feet, to drive forward with their arms rather than across their bodies. Their knees should rise to 90 degrees, and their heads be kept upright.

DYNAMIC AND STATIC STRETCHING

(see sessions 4, 11, 13, 20)

Stretching becomes increasingly important as players get older and is a good habit to instil in young players.

Dynamic stretching can be used before your sessions or matches and **static** stretching after a session or match. Dynamic stretching is a progressive stretch through a specific range of movement, with the end position being held for one or two seconds then repeated. The idea is to replicate the movements that players will use during a session or a match. Dynamic stretching will also increase a player's core temperature, which can improve performance and reduce injury risk.

Static stretching, where a stretch is held for more than 20 seconds, can be used after an activity to assist with recovery, injury management and maintaining flexibility.

Examples of dynamic stretches include lunges, squats, also known as 'sumos', hamstring and calf stretches, knees at 90 degrees moving 'up and out', to loosen groin muscles, side stretches, bicep and tricep stretches. All are done on the move. Demonstrations are important to ensure safe and accurate stretching by the players.

A good way to conduct a dynamic stretch warm-up is to start the drills in a line, moving together as fast as your slowest man. It is good for teamwork as well, because players have to judge how fast to move and maintain a consistent pace and line.

Andrew Flintoff goes through a pre-match routine.

WARM-UP GAMES
Piggy in the middle (see session 3)
Set-up and equipment: This is best for a small group of six or eight players using a 10m × 10m grid. Tennis balls.

How it works: One player is nominated as 'piggy', and it is the job of the other players to keep the ball away from him. You are not allowed to hold the ball for more than three seconds. You are not allowed to run with the ball, go out of the grid or stop running if you don't have the ball. If you do, you become the next 'piggy'.

Coaching aim: Communication, movement and catching under pressure.

Stuck in the mud

Set-up and equipment: A 10m × 10m grid. Bibs. Tennis balls.

How it works: Two or three nominated players each have a ball in their hand. Like in tag, the other players are trying to get away from the guys with the balls. If they are touched by the ball they stand still with their arms outstretched. If someone runs under their arms then they are freed and can carry on running. This game is especially enjoyed by the youngest players.

Coaching aim: Replicating movements you would use in a match situation.

Hand hockey (see sessions 2, 16)

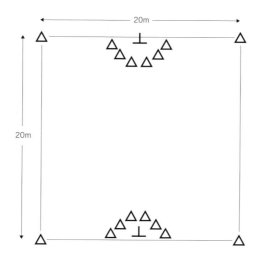

Set-up and equipment: Four cones are the corners of your playing area, maybe 20m × 20m. Bibs to identify teams. Then set up a stump at each end. The stump is the equivalent of a goal. Form a D with cones around the stump. The game is played with a tennis ball or an IncrediBall®.

How it works: Split your group into two teams. The aim is to score a point or a goal by hitting the stump. Players must pass the ball to their team members. They cannot run with the ball and have only three seconds before having to pass it. Once a player in possession is close to the D he can attempt an underarm throw at the stump. No player is allowed in the D. The opposing team is trying to intercept the passes and acquire possession of the ball.

Coaching aim: Picking up cleanly, hand-eye coordination.

Vortex (see sessions 5, 20)

Set-up and equipment: A 20m × 20m grid. Players split into two equal teams with bibs to identify.

How it works: Players move around while throwing the vortex to their team-mates. The first team to catch ten passes in a row is the winner. A variation is to stipulate a number of passes that you have to complete before you can attempt to score a point, which you do by passing to one of your team-mates who is behind an end-line.

Coaching aim: Moving into space, catching under pressure.

Dodgeball (last man stands) (see sessions 6, 12)

Set-up and equipment: One team in the middle of a circle of cones, one team on the outside of the circle. Use tennis balls or soft balls, nothing harder than a tennis ball.

How it works: The idea is to eliminate the people in the middle of the circle. There are three key rules: 1. You can only throw from outside the circle, 2. You can only throw below waist height, and 3. You can only throw underarm. If you are hit then you leave the circle and join the throwing group. The last person left inside the circle is the winner.

Alternative: Team dodgeball against the clock. You can see how long one team can survive. If a player is out then they do not join the throwing group to try to get their team-mates out, they just step aside and then you swap around when each team has finished.

Coaching aim: Players can learn the importance of backing up in the field: those on the far side of the circle should be alert to throws coming from team-mates that do not find their intended target and pass through the circle.

One-bounce box game (see sessions 9, 19)

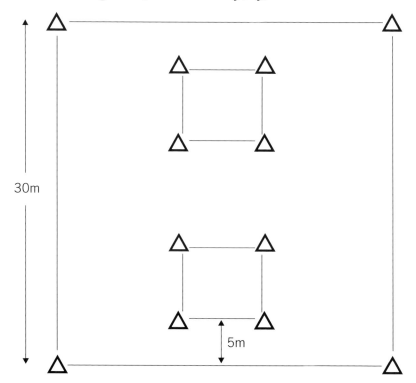

Set-up and equipment: A 30m × 30m grid. Two teams with bibs. Tennis ball or similar.

How it works: You are not allowed to run with the ball but you can run off the ball. You can keep possession of the ball for three seconds. You have to pass it to your team-mates by bouncing once on the ground. To score a point you have to bounce it once into an opposition coned-off area (4m × 4m) inside the main grid and one of your team-mates has to catch it on the other side. No player is allowed inside the scoring box.

Coaching aim: Catching and movement.

CATCHING DRILLS
Basic catching

If you are working with a particularly young or inexperienced group, or perhaps are working with a group for the first time and are unsure about their level of ability, you can start with a very basic catching drill and quickly develop according to ability. This is also a good way of introducing a hard ball to players who have not experienced it before, as it allows them to feel and catch the ball in an easy and safe way.

Set-up and equipment: A ball for each player. Players spread out so they are not in each other's way.

How it works: Just let each player throw the ball up and catch it. Then you can encourage them to walk around a bit while throwing the ball up and catching it. If players are unable to do that, they should throw the ball a very close distance. The more confident ones can throw a little higher.

Progression: Players jog around while catching and throwing. Next players clap while the ball is in the air and increase the number of claps before they catch it. Next players throw the ball up, touch two hands on the ground, stand up and catch it. Next players throw the ball up, turn 360 degrees and catch the ball. These latter progressions are not easy!

Coaching aim: Watching the ball.

Catching and throwing in pairs

Set-up and equipment: Split your group into pairs with one ball per pair. Each pair of players stands opposite each other. They can begin close together, maybe only a metre or two apart, depending on ability, and gradually move further apart.

How it works: Players start by throwing gentle underarm catches to each other in their pairs, progressing the difficulty of it by making the throws harder or moving the players further apart from each other. You can then introduce a competition element, whereby if one player drops the ball three times the other partner in the pair wins. The throws must be reasonably accurate of course. If the receiver has to move more than two steps then that goes against the thrower and he loses a life.

Coaching aim: Hand position: fingers pointing down for any catch up to stomach height; fingers pointing up for chest height and above.

Indian legend Sachin Tendulkar catching a head-high ball with fingers pointing upwards.

Wall catching (see session 13)

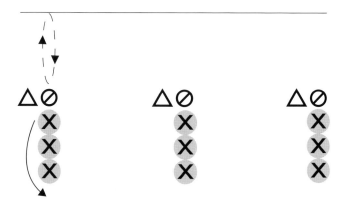

Set-up and equipment: Players split into three groups behind three cones. Tennis balls.

How it works: Player at the front of the queue underarms the ball at the wall and moves out of the way to his left to go to the back of the queue. Next player in line catches the ball and repeats.

Progression: 1. Use overarm throws and move the players further from the wall as appropriate. 2. Now the players' bravery will be tested. The first player underarms the ball at the wall as before but waits until the last moment before moving out of the way. This means the catcher behind him has very little time to react. If the thrower is hit by the ball he is out of the competition, as is the catcher if he drops the ball. Play a last-man stands game until there is one player left from each group. Then they play against each other in a grand final.

Coaching aim: Getting into a good set position so the player is ready to make a catch or move out of the way.

Pairs catching

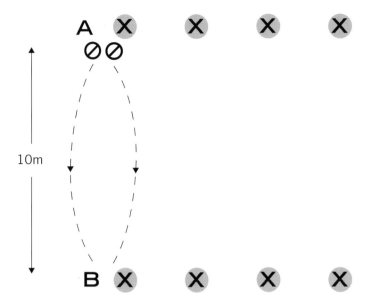

Set-up and equipment: Use tennis balls only. Players line up in pairs 10m apart.

How it works: Player A has two tennis balls and underarms them to Player B from the same hand at the same time. B attempts to catch both balls.

Coaching aim: Developing peripheral vision.

Diagonal move and catch

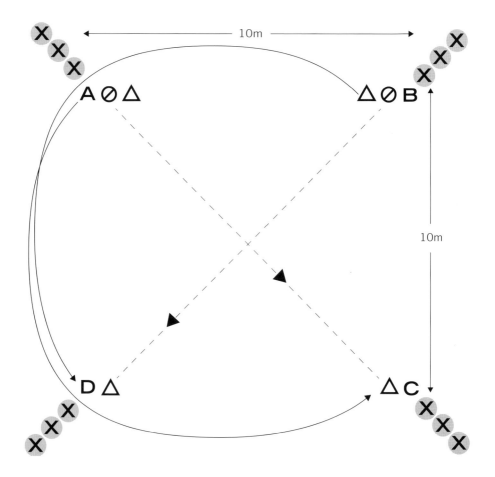

10m

10m

A ⊘ △

△ ⊘ B

D △

△ C

Set-up and equipment: Teams are split evenly on the four points of the grid, roughly 10m by 10m. Teams work diagonally across the grid. A cone at each corner of the grid. Two balls.

How it works: To begin with, A rolls the ball underarm along the ground to C and C picks up. A moves anti-clockwise to the back of the queue at C and the new player at C rolls to A and so on. Alternatives are for A to throw a catch to C, for A to bounce the ball once to C, or for A to throw the ball at shoulder height to C. B and D do the same at the same time.

Progression: Add fitness equipment such as ladders or hurdles at each cone. Players have to complete these obstacles before being in a position to catch or throw the ball.

Coaching aim: Communication, catching and throwing on the move.

Fast throw and catch (see session 14)

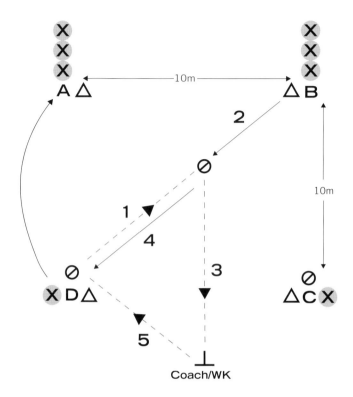

Set-up and equipment: Players line up at points A and B on the grid, with one player each at C and D. Teams are split evenly on the four points of a 10m × 10m grid. Four cones, one ball, one stump.

How it works: It is a fast-paced game with the ball being moved around quickly. D rolls the ball to B, who advances to attack the ball: D goes to the back of A after rolling the ball. B picks up, underarms a throw to the coach, or your team's wicketkeeper, and then moves to position D, where the coach pops a catch to him so he can roll the ball out. Then C rolls to A, who attacks the ball and throws to the coach. The players queuing up at points A and B take it in turns to receive the ball. The coach should orchestrate the drill by shouting A or B depending on whose turn it is. The ideal scenario is for all the actions to be done slickly and quickly to improve reaction times, concentration and fielding under pressure.

Coaching aim: Concentration and focus; combining different skills within the same drill.

Short catching

1.

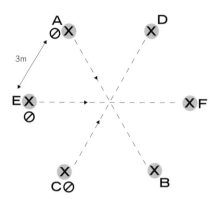

2.

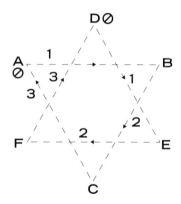

Set-up and equipment: Six players in a circle about 3m apart. Three balls.

How it works: 1. Players with a ball underarm the ball to their opposite man across the circle – A to B, etc. – simultaneously. They face the challenge of the distraction of there being three balls in the air at any time, so players must concentrate well and keep focus. 2. Players at A and B have a ball each and this time throw round the circle anti-clockwise but missing out the player to their immediate left. So A throws to B who throws to C; D to E to F.

Progression: 1. Players have to catch one-handed or use their weaker hand to catch and throw. 2. Then they have to change direction and the balls go back the other way.

Coaching aim: Each player focusing on his own ball, not getting distracted.

Flat catches

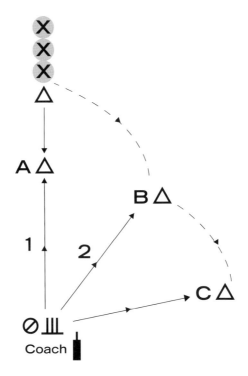

Set-up and equipment: Stump and four cones. Coach with a bat. Players line up behind point A.

How it works: The first player walks forward, sets himself like a goalkeeper in football and the coach hits a flat catch (stomach height) to him, which he returns to the coach. He moves left to B and receives another flat catch, and then on to C for the same. He then runs round the back of the coach to join the back of the queue.

Progression: Speed up the drill. Introduce a fitness and movement station such as a ladder or some hurdles before the first catching point.

Coaching aim: To take clean catches with good technique: a solid base and fingers pointing to the ground, giving a large catching area.

Catching tough

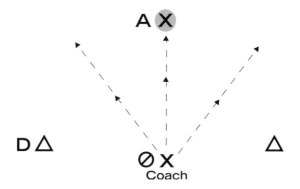

Set-up and equipment: Cones, balls. This is ideal for a smaller group.

How it works: Coach gives 10 catches to one player who starts at point A but is moved around a 10m × 10m grid by the direction of the catches. Other players are resting, waiting their turn.

Progression: Add a second ball so that the catcher is never allowed to settle.

Coaching aim: Fast feet, catching on the move, endurance.

Reaction catches

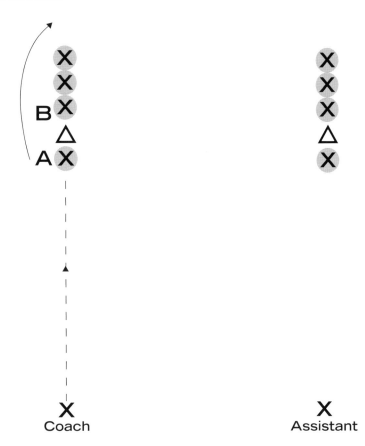

Set-up and equipment: Soft balls to be used but all players should wear helmets and a box. Cones at the four points of a 10m × 10m grid. One player stands in front of the cone in both lines while others line up behind.

How it works: The coach underarms at A between waist and head height. A moves out of the way at the last moment for B, whose view has been obstructed, to catch the ball. A moves to the back of the queue and B moves forward to obstruct.

Coaching aim: Developing good reaction speed.

Group catching competition (see session 4)

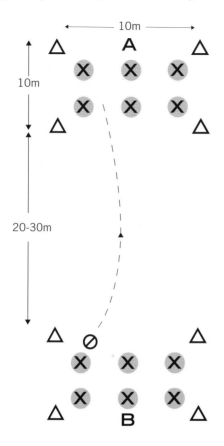

Set-up and equipment: Players split into equal teams. Two 10m × 10m grids set around 20–30m apart, depending on ability. For younger or less experienced players the two grids can be closer together. Use tennis balls.

How it works: Players arrange themselves evenly inside their allotted grid. The first player in team A has to throw the ball overarm into team B's grid. If the ball does not land within the grid then that player is out of the game. As the ball approaches team B the player closest to the ball must call his name and attempt to catch the ball. If he does not call or drops the ball, he is out. The winner of the game is the last player standing. Younger or less experienced players can throw underarm if required.

Coaching aim: Communication; learning to call for the ball which will be required in a match if two players are close to the same catch.

Diving catches

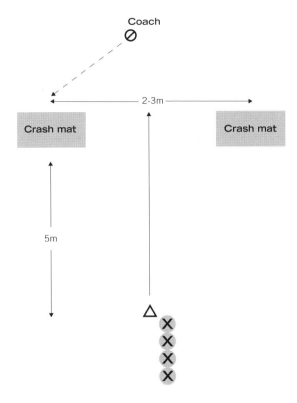

Coach

2-3m

Crash mat   Crash mat

5m

Set-up and equipment: Soft dive mats as commonly found in a school gym. It is important that these are the large, soft ones and not the thinner, harder ones, which are not safe for this drill. Two mats are placed 2–3m apart. Soft or hard balls can be used for this drill.

How it works: The first player walks in hard to the space between the crash mats. The coach throws a ball at an angle at one of the mats, the player dives and attempts to take a two-handed catch. He returns the ball to the coach before returning to the back of the queue. It is important that the players are lined up a safe distance away and also not in the line of the coach's throws.

Progression: The coach throws the ball on to a reaction board to make the catches more challenging.

Coaching aim: Fast feet; learning how to land after taking the catch, that is not on the pointed parts of the body, such as the knees or elbows.

Reaction board catching

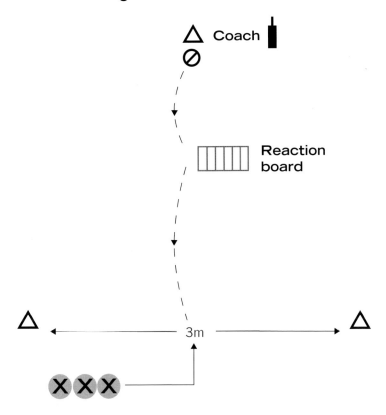

Set-up and equipment: Two cones, reaction board and a small bat for the coach. This is one for more experienced players.

How it works: Player steps up into line with the two cones and sets himself for a catch. The coach hits the ball down on to the reaction board, causing the ball to fly towards the catcher at an unpredictable angle. Players waiting their turn need to be in a safe area and not directly in the line of the balls.

Coaching aim: Develop reaction and reflex catching.

Bowling-machine catching

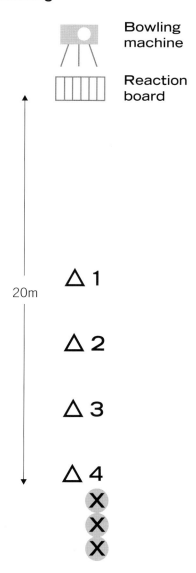

Set-up and equipment: Bowling machine on its short legs. Reaction board. Tennis balls. Four cones spaced in a line moving back from the reaction board around 20m. This is one for older or more experienced players. And for a coach who is familiar enough with using a bowling machine. Ensure that the set-up is safe: that the speed on the bowling machine is appropriate to the level of player (see bowling machine information on page 96). Try out beforehand. Start slowly and build up if necessary.

How it works: Players start at cone 4, taking three (or more) catches fired from the bowling machine, then progress through the other cones taking three catches at each station. Cone 1 should be a very challenging reaction catch.

Progression: Increase the speed of the bowling machine, moving the cones closer. Introduce a competitive element.

Coaching aim: Develop reaction and reflex catching.

England's Ian Bell has his reactions tested to the full.

FIELDING DRILLS
Short fielding (see session 11)

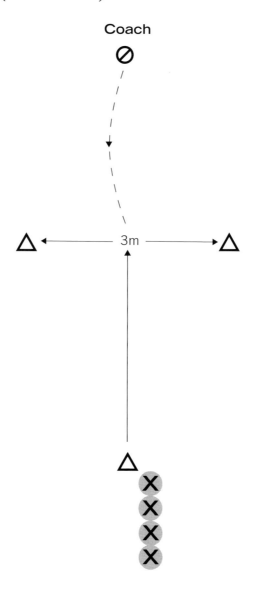

Coach

3m

Set-up and equipment: Two cones. Reaction board. Tennis racket. Hard and soft balls.

How it works: Player walks in hard between the two cones and sets himself for either a roll-out from the coach, a soft-ball catch via the tennis racket, or a hard-ball catch from the reaction board. He returns the ball to the coach and returns to the back of the queue.

Coaching aim: Getting into a good set position, like a goalkeeper.

Boundary fielding (see session 11)

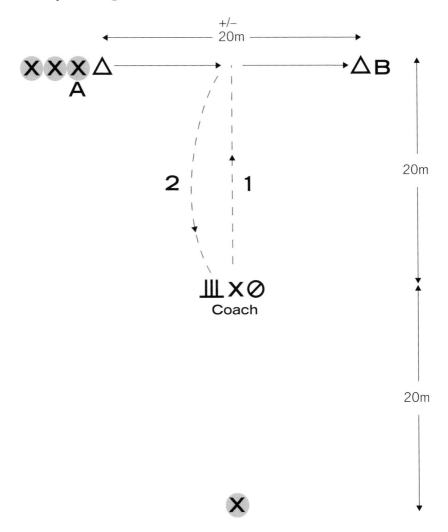

Set-up and equipment: Two cones set up about 20m apart. The coach stands by a stump (or set of stumps) about 20m away between the two cones. 20m behind the coach is a player to back-up the throws. Players line up at A.

How it works: The coach rolls the ball between A and B, the first player in the line fields the ball using the long barrier method and returns the ball with an overarm throw to the coach. A good way of speeding up this drill is to use more than one ball so that you are not waiting for a wayward throw to be returned to you before continuing the drill. The thrower moves round to replace the back-up player. Repeat the drill with players lining up at B and moving from left to right.

Coaching aim: Players should have no gaps in their barrier and ensure their barrier position allows them to get into a throwing position quickly. Right-handed throwers should field the ball with their left knee touching the ground, and vice versa for a left-handed thrower.

Throwing in pairs (see session 2)

Set-up and equipment: Players working in pairs across the sports hall/practice area using soft balls.

How it works: Players throw to each other overarm.

Coaching aim: Players should stay side-on and keep their front arm high.

Underarm stump aim (see session 10)

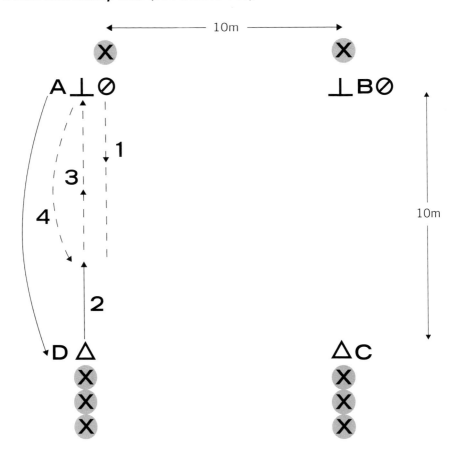

Set-up and equipment: One player with a ball at points A and B, the rest split equally at C and D. Two cones and two single stumps or two sets of stumps. The stumps should be set up at points A and B on the grid.

How it works: A rolls the ball to D, who attacks the ball and underarms it back to A. A then pops up a catch to D, who replaces A at the stump. A joins the back of the queue at D. Same takes place simultaneously with B and C.

Progression: Add a fitness ladder to points D and C.

Coaching aim: Reacting to the height of the ball.

Underarm stump competition

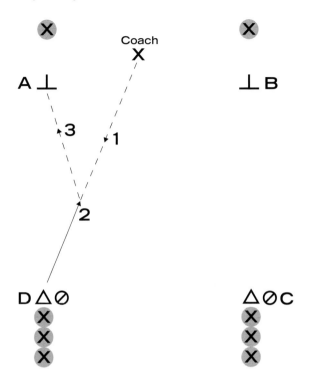

Set-up and equipment: As in the previous drill, but with the coach standing between A and B. Use only IncrediBalls® or tennis balls, not cricket balls.

How it works: Coach rolls the ball to D, who attacks the ball and attempts to hit the stump (A) with an underarm throw. The player at A is positioned well behind the stump to collect the ball if it misses the stump. If D does miss the stump he returns to his starting point, does one press-up and has another attempt. When he hits the stump, he replaces A, who goes to the back of the queue at D. Each team takes alternate attempts. When each player has hit the stump once you then run the drill as a competition, with the team that hits the stump 10 times being the winner.

Alternative: Use a full set of three stumps, which is useful for less experienced or younger players. When you make it into a competition you can play the first to three hits, but remove one stump each time a player hits.

Coaching aim: Staying low to pick the ball up; competing under pressure.

Mixed-up catch and roll

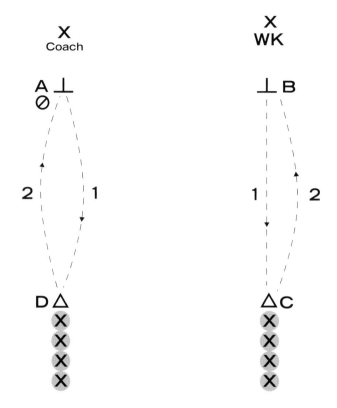

Set-up and equipment: Two balls, two sets of stumps or two single stumps, wicketkeeping gloves, mitt for the coach. Coach at point A, wicketkeeper at B, two teams split equally at C and D.

How it works: Coach pops **underarm catches** to the first player in the line at D. D catches and returns the ball to the coach and joins the back of the queue at D. The wicketkeeper **rolls the ball** on the ground to C, who attacks the ball and throws it back to the keeper. After a period of time C and D swap places.

Coaching aim: Staying low to pick up the ball.

Intercept and throw

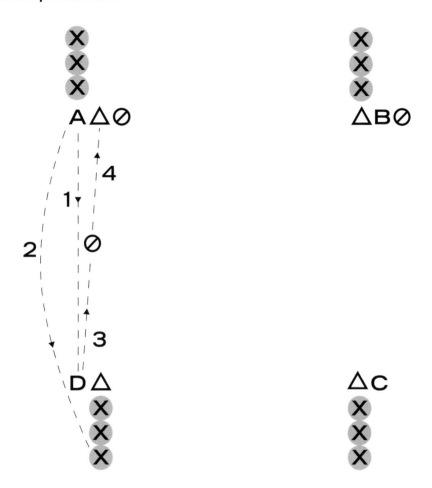

Set-up and equipment: Teams split equally at the four cones. Two balls.

How it works: A rolls the ball on the ground to D. A joins the back of the queue at D. D attacks A's roll and rolls it for the next player. B and C do the same.

Progression: Players pick up the ball using their strong hand, but roll it or throw it back using their weaker hand. Another option is to have players using only their weaker hands. You can adapt the roll and the throw to include a one-bounce throw or a pop-up catch.

Coaching aim: Developing use of weaker hands.

Diagonal throw and move

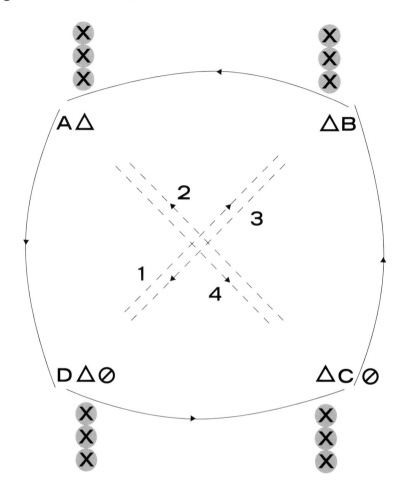

Set-up and equipment: As for 'Intercept and throw' (previous page). Use only tennis balls or Incrediballs®.

How it works: D rolls or throws underarm to B and runs to the back of C. C underarms to A, who runs to the back of B. B underarms to D, who runs to the back of A. A underarms to C, who runs to the back of D.

Progression: 1. Take the cones back five steps and work on overarm throws. 2. Make players use their weaker hands to pick up and throw.

Coaching aim: Movement, clean pick-ups under pressure.

Direct hits

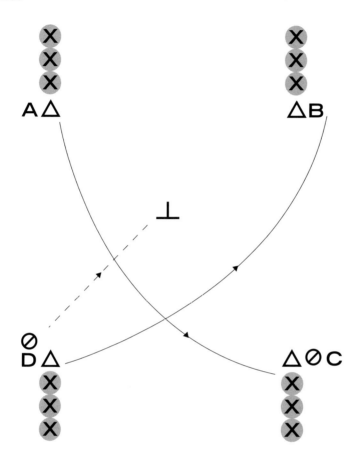

Set-up and equipment: As for 'Diagonal throw and move' (previous page), but this time add a single stump in the middle of a 10m × 10m grid to work on direct hits. Ball each at C and D.

How it works: As for 'Diagonal throw and move', but players aim their under-arm throws at the stump, and then move to the back of their respective queues.

Progression: To introduce a fitness and competitive element, players must run around the outside of the grid to get to the back of their assigned queue. A and C form one team, B and D the other. So C would move to the back of A and D to the back of B etc. Another progression is to introduce overarm throws.

Coaching aim: Fitness; staying low to pick up the ball.

Throw and back-up

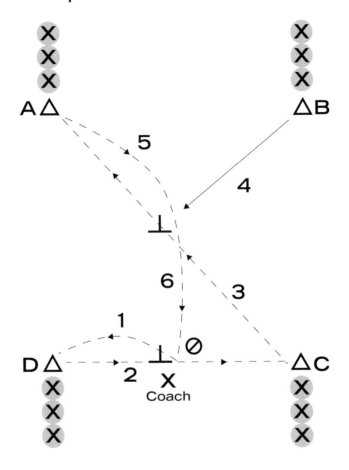

Set-up and equipment: Two stumps, one ball. Players split equally at the four corners of a 10m × 10m grid.

How it works: Coach hits a catch to D. D rolls the ball at the coach's stump. The coach lets the ball roll past him (the game is interrupted if the ball hits the stump) and on to C, who backs up and collects the ball. C underarms at the stump in the middle of the grid. A backs up C's throw and underarms to B, who has moved to the middle stump to collect A's throw. B throws back to the coach. Every player moves one space to the right and goes to the back of the queue.

Coaching aim: To create and improve understanding of the importance of backing-up throws in the field and also the need for a fielder to move to the stumps, when vacant, during a run-out opportunity.

Pick-up from the side

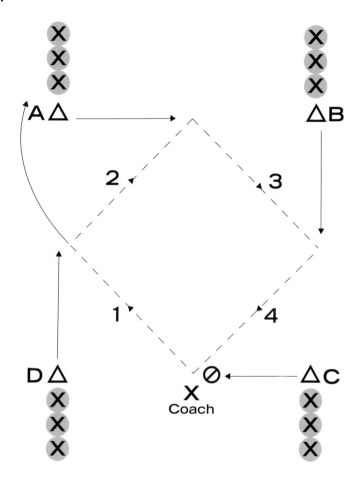

Set-up and equipment: Players split equally at the four corners of a 10m × 10m grid. One ball to start with.

How it works: Coach rolls the ball between A and D. D picks the ball up on the run and then rolls the ball between A and B. A picks up on the run and rolls between B and C. B picks up on the run and rolls between C and D, etc. Players move anticlockwise round the grid, so D joins the back of A, etc.

Progression: Instead of rolling the ball, make it a catch. Add an additional ball to make it faster, and have more players moving at any one time.

Coaching aim: Picking up on the move.

Diagonal throw

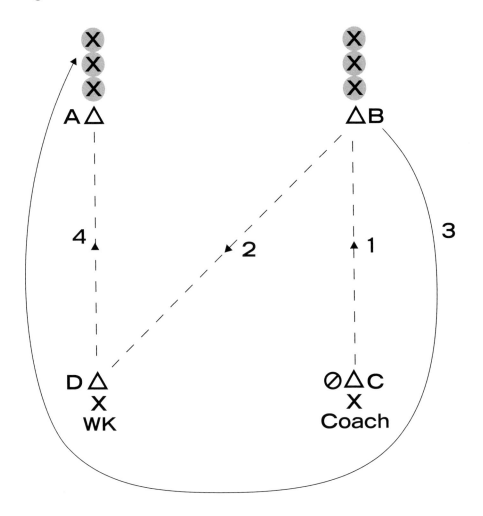

Set-up and equipment: Players split between points A and B, except for a wicketkeeper at D.

How it works: Coach rolls the ball out straight to B. B collects the ball and underarms a return to the wicketkeeper. B runs around the outside of the grid to the back of the queue at A. The keeper then rolls to A, who collects and returns to the coach. The process continues alternating between A and B.

Coaching aim: Staying low to pick up the ball.

Run-outs

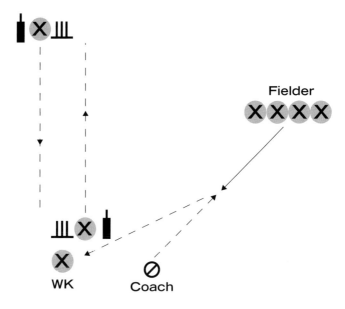

Set-up and equipment: Two sets of stumps. Two teams, one batting, one fielding. Batting team is split into pairs. Fielding team lines up around 20m to the side of the batting stumps.

How it works: Coach rolls the ball towards the first player on the fielding team, who attacks the ball and underarms it to the wicketkeeper. The batting pairs try to complete a single run before the ball is returned. The team that scores the most runs wins.

Coaching aim: Fielding under pressure.

Pass and follow

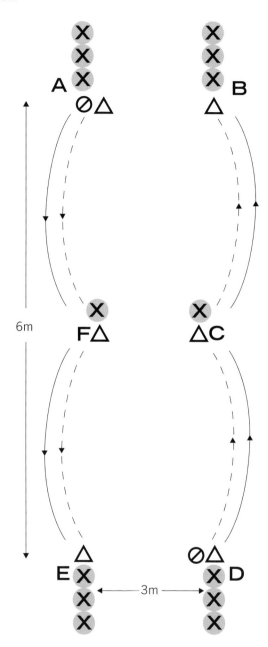

Set-up and equipment: A grid roughly 6m × 3m, with cones at the four corners and two midway down the longer sides of the grid. Players line up at the four corners with one each at points C and F.

How it works: Players at A and D each have a ball and the idea is that they pass, via a sharp underarm throw, anticlockwise to the next player round the grid. When they have passed the ball the player then follows it (e.g. D runs round to C). But players must turn quickly to be aware of where the next ball is coming from. If a player simply throws the ball and admires the pass then he will be unaware of when the next throw is coming his way. When a player has completed a circuit he goes to back of the queue where he started from.

Progression: You can introduce more balls or make them change direction. You can specify which hand they are allowed to use or specify only their weaker hand. You can specify low or high catches.

Coaching aim: Concentration and awareness.

Backing up

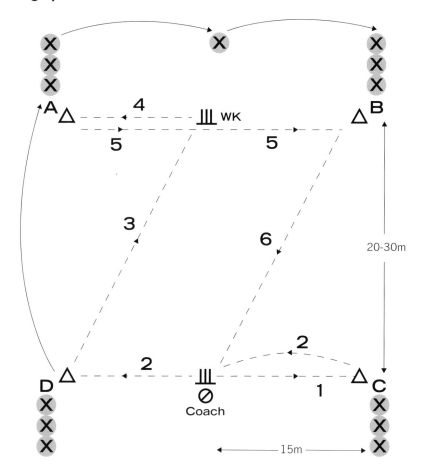

Set-up and equipment: Two sets of stumps and four cones. Players line up equally at points A to D. Coach is positioned at one set of stumps and either a wicketkeeper or an assistant is at the other.

How it works: Coach rolls to C, who attacks the ball and throws at the coach's stumps. The coach lets the ball pass, where B is ready to back up. D throws overarm to the keeper. The keeper rolls to A, who throws at the stumps. B backs up and throws overarm to the coach. Every player moves one place to the left and to the back of the queue. Players moving from A to B and C to D should back up the throws coming from B and D respectively.

Coaching aim: Attacking the ball, throwing and awareness of backing-up.

Relay fielding (see session 17)

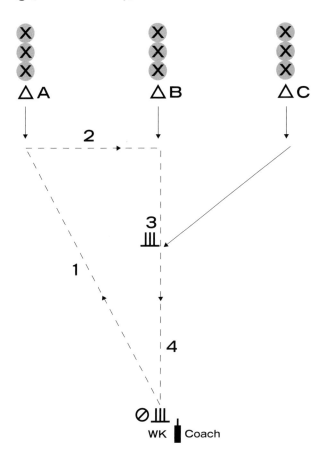

Set-up and equipment: Three cones, two sets of stumps and ideally a wicket-keeper or an assistant. Coach has a bat.

How it works: Players work in threes. The coach hits the ball out to any one of the three stations. For example, A receives the ball and will pass it to B. C moves to the first set of stumps. He receives the ball from B and throws it the keeper. The three players then return to the back of the queues and the drill is repeated with the next set of players. If B receives the ball then he passes it to C and A goes to the stumps. If C receives it he passes to A and B goes to the stumps. Keeping the sequence the same (i.e. A–B–C) ensures clarity for all.

Coaching aim: Fielders work together and learn the benefit of relay throwing to make retrievals from close to the boundary more efficient.

Advanced relay fielding

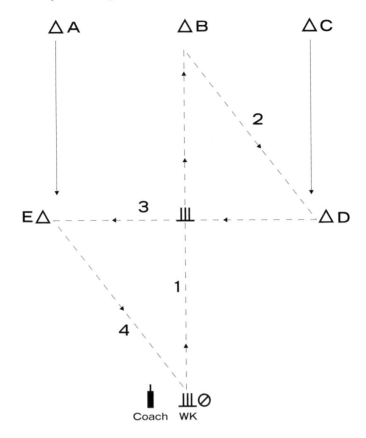

Set-up and equipment: Similar to 'Relay fielding' (see previous page) but two extra cones are positioned level with the first set of stumps in front of A and B.

How it works: Coach always hits down the middle to B. C runs to D and receives a throw from B. A runs to E and receives a throw from C. A throws to the wicketkeeper. Every player returns to the back of the queues but moves one place to the left: A to B, B to C, C to A.

Progression: Introduce a direct hit at the first set of stumps from C, with A backing up before A returns the ball to the keeper.

Coaching aim: Teamwork and alertness, similar to the relay fielding.

Team relay fielding (see session 8)

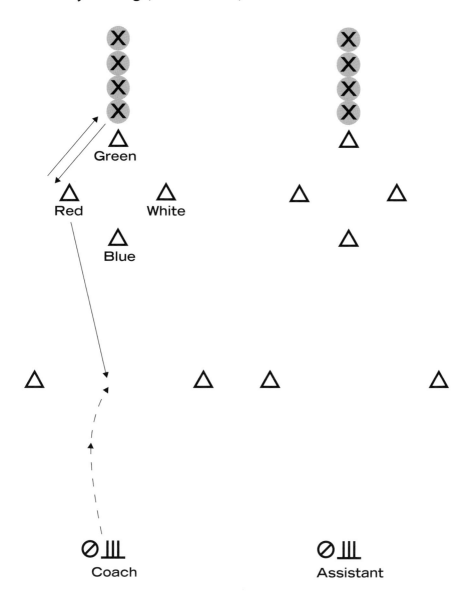

Set-up and equipment: Players split into two teams and line up behind a diamond arrangement of four coloured cones. Two cones act as a gate or finishing line. The coach (and hopefully an assistant) stands with balls at a set of stumps.

How it works: The coach calls a sequence of colours, e.g. 'Red, red', and the first player runs to red, touches the cone and returns, then goes again to red, back to the start, and then runs through the gate which is initially a finish line but will become a gateway to the fielding element of the drill. He returns to the back of his team queue and the next player on his team goes.

Progression: Introduce fielding elements. 1. The gate is no longer a finish line but the place at which the player fields a ball rolled to him by the coach. He throws at the stumps and if he hits he scores a point for his team. 2. Or when he comes through the gate he could set himself and then be thrown a flat catch. He returns it to the coach, runs round the coach and runs back through the gate, but as he is returning the coach rolls the ball again and he has to pick up, turn and throw at the stumps. 3. Instead of the coach being the one to throw and receive, have a player as the ball feeder who is replaced by the player who has just completed the drill. Fitness and movement hurdles or ladders can be added after they come out of the cones. Teams are trying to complete each variant of the drill as quickly as possible and beat their opponents.

Coaching aim: Fielding under pressure and encouraging good movement.

Run-out competition

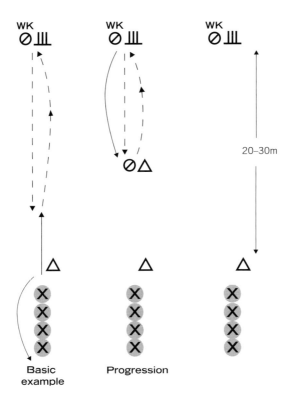

Basic example

Progression

WK

WK

WK

20–30m

Set-up and equipment: Players split into three teams. Three sets of stumps. Three cones 20–30m away from the stumps. Each team nominates a wicket-keeper. Keepers must be fully padded up if hard balls are to be used.

How it works: On the coach's command, the wicketkeeper rolls the ball out towards the cones, the first player attacks the ball and throws overarm to the stop of the stumps. The keeper catches the ball and touches the stumps. The first keeper to do this scores a point for his team. First team to 10 wins. The keeper can only roll the ball out and must release the ball only on the coach's command.

Progression: Once the player has thrown into the keeper, he sprints round the back of his own keeper. The keepers roll out again, the players pick up the ball and throw on the turn. A cone would need to be set to indicate the minimum distance the keeper has to roll the ball to once the player has run behind him.

Coaching aim: Fielding under pressure.

Wicketkeeping drill (see session 15)

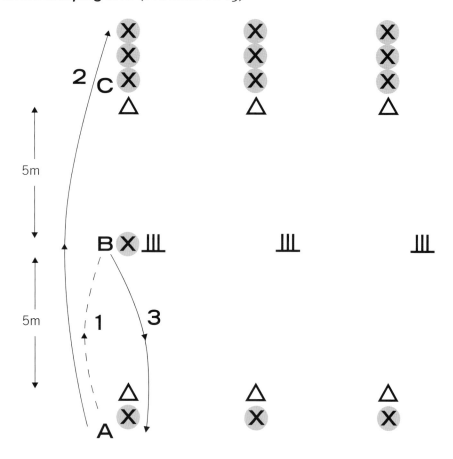

Set-up and equipment: Three sets of stumps and six cones. Players split into three teams. Use tennis balls or IncrediBalls®. Although this is focused on wicketkeeping skills it is a drill for everyone. The wicketkeepers in your group can wear their gloves if they choose. The players at B should be in wicketkeeping mode (see Coaching aim) How it works: A throws the ball to B, who takes the catch and touches the stumps. A runs round to the back of the queue at C. B moves forward to take the place of A. The next in line at C comes forward to the wicketkeeping position at B. The first team to take 25 clean catches is the winner.

Progression: 1. Introduce a batsman at the stumps. The batsman will not hit the ball but play a 'ghost' shot to make it harder for the keeper. 2. Vary the angle of the throws from A to make it harder for the keeper. You can judge how far to push this depending on how easy or hard the players find the initial drill.

Coaching aim: Wicketkeeping technique: feet shoulder-width apart, fingers spread touching the floor, hands together, head behind the line of the ball, on the balls of the feet and rising with the ball.

England Test keeper Matt Prior shows good balance and concentration.

BATTING DRILLS AND GAMES

6.

Don Bradman famously honed his batting technique by hitting a golf ball with a cricket stump against a cylindrical water tank so the ball would come off at unpredictable angles. There are many unconventional ways to practise hitting a ball. A ball in a stocking suspended from the branch of a tree or maybe a convenient spot in a garage is great for an individual to groove his batting away from formalised team practice sessions.

There really is no substitute for well-structured, focused and intense practice. But this chapter concentrates on the more conventional ways to coach batting in a group, whether that be in an open area (sports hall or outside) or in the nets. At the most basic level, there are the different ways that a coach, or indeed a team-mate, can feed the ball to a batsman for practice. Then there are drills to learn and groove certain shots. There are also games that incorporate the skills learned into a fun competition. There is no need to over-complicate drills and activities. You will still see the top international batsmen practising their shots with a simple drop feed from a coach or a throw-down from a team-mate.

There are many examples and options presented in this book, but the best players will always return to the basics. Your job as a coach is to keep it simple and encourage players to develop understanding of their own game.

The principles of fun, safety, maximum participation and achievement should always be applied. Safety information about protective equipment for junior players and bowling machine usage is also included.

The coaching aims that accompany the explanations of each drill are examples to aid the coach. They are not necessarily the only technical elements involved in the execution of a particular shot or skill.

WAYS TO FEED THE BALL TO A BATSMAN FOR DRILLS

Hitting off a tee

The entry-level way to practise batting. The ball is hit off a stationary tee. This method can be used for most shots, including back-foot shots like the pull, where the tee can be placed on top of a stump.

Drop feed

The feeder (team-mate or coach) stands to the off side of the batsman a safe distance away, ensuring he is not in any danger from the batsman playing his shot. The ball is dropped from an outstretched arm and the batsman should aim to hit the ball on the second bounce. Good for practising driving the ball.

Bobble feed

The feeder stands 10–15m in front of the batsman and rolls the ball towards him so that it bounces twice or more. Good for practising driving. If the lofted drive is to be practised then the feeder should ensure he is a safe enough distance away to avoid the airborne ball.

Cheek drop

Batsman places the ball between his cheek and his front shoulder. He tilts his head upright to let the ball drop and drives the ball on the second bounce.

Throw-downs

Feeder stands in front of the batsman a similar distance away as for the bobble feed, and throws overarm to the batsman. The length of delivery can be adjusted depending on what sort of shot is to be practised. This is a good way to practise shots off the front and back foot.

BATTING BASICS, BALANCE AND REACTION SPEED

Batting set-up (see session 1)

Set-up and equipment: Every player is positioned with a bat and ideally a set of stumps, though this is unlikely to be practical. One option is to split into pairs, with one player batting (in front of a set of stumps) and one observing. Then the players swap after a few minutes.

How it works: Batsmen go through their pre-delivery set-up with special focus on five key areas: 1. Maintaining an upright head position, 2. Keeping the eyes level, 3. Feet roughly shoulder-width apart to stay balanced, 4. Picking the bat up over off stump, 5. The importance of establishing a guard so the batsman knows where his off stump is and can judge which balls to defend, attack or leave. The simplest place to start is to suggest a middle-stump guard. Batsmen will develop their own personal preferences as they progress.

Coaching aim: Focus on balance and the importance of establishing a firm base. More information can be introduced when this drill is revisited.

Head to line (see session 16)

Set-up and equipment: Players work in pairs. One player is set in his batting position but without a bat. Soft balls.

How it works: The batsman's partner feeds him underarm throws and he moves late towards the ball to catch it as if he were going to play a shot. Feed six balls and then swap with partner.

Coaching aim: Look for the head leading the movement towards the ball.

Bean-bag balance (see session 16)

Set-up and equipment: Players work in pairs. One soft ball and one bean-bag per pair.

How it works: One drop-feeds six balls to his partner who plays a front-foot drive with a bean-bag on his head.

Coaching aim: To maintain still head position and balance.

Bench batting (see session 16)

Set-up and equipment: Batsmen work in pairs, one pair per bench.

How it works: One player sets up a ball on a tee for the batsman to hit. Swap after six hits. This also works with a drop feed.

Coaching aim: To develop balance.

Front-foot isolation
(see session 16)

Set-up and equipment: Batsmen work in pairs, one ball per pair.

How it works: The batsman hits shots being fed underarm, similar to a bobble feed, by his partner while standing only on his front foot.

Coaching aim: Excellent for developing good balance and head position.

Duck and swerve (see session 16)

Set-up and equipment: Batsmen work in pairs. Tennis balls. Helmets essential.

How it works: The batsman receives tennis ball feeds at head height and attempts to duck or sway out of the way. The ball can be fed either underarm from a standing position or on the bounce from a kneeling position.

Coaching aim: The batsman has to watch the ball closely all the way. As soon as a batsman turns his head away from the ball he is in trouble.

Wall work (see session 16)

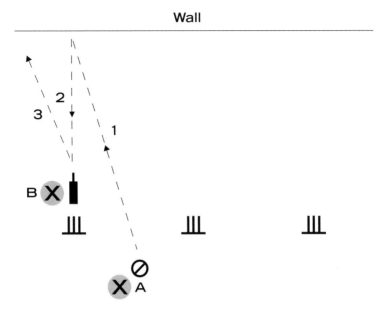

Set-up and equipment: Players in pairs. One with a bat, one with a ball. Six sets of stumps or cones. Tennis balls. Helmets must be worn and players made aware of safety. If this drill is used for pull shots then you must ensure there are no other players in the batsman's hitting line.

How it works: B is facing the wall in batting position as if facing a bowler. A throws the ball underarm at the wall. B plays the ball as it rebounds from the wall. Players swap places after six deliveries.

Progression: A uses two differently coloured balls. One ball is nominated to receive a defensive shot, the other an attacking shot. The batsman does not know in advance which ball will be received. It can also be an overarm feed to speed up the drill.

Coaching aim: Developing hand-eye coordination and reaction speed.

Reaction board feed

Set-up and equipment: Reaction board set up between the batsman and a feeder.

How it works: The feeder, on one knee, skims a throw off a reaction board towards the batsman.

Coaching aim: The batsman is forced to play the ball late.

Off-stump awareness

Set-up and equipment: Two sets of stumps set up next to each other to create a wicket of six stumps.

How it works: Batsman receives a bobble feed and after playing a shot has to comment on which stump (of the six) the ball would have hit. Tip: this drill works best in a one-to-one situation. If you have a number of assistants or coaches on hand then it can be made into a group activity.

Coaching aim: As the name of the drill suggests, the batsman learns where his off stump is.

SPECIFIC BATTING SHOTS
Lofted or front-foot drive (see session 6)

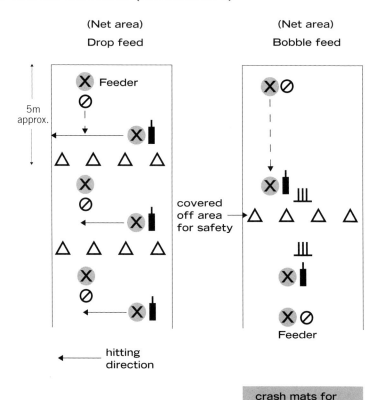

Set-up and equipment: Players work in pairs using tennis balls. You should comfortably be able to have three pairs per net, a safe distance apart, hitting into the side of the net. Ensure that the batsmen in adjoining nets are hitting in opposite directions.

How it works: The batsman receives a drop feed from his partner (he must stand to the off side of the batsman for safety reasons) and hits a drive off the front foot on the second bounce. Batsmen should hit six balls then swap with their partner. Batsmen should receive three sets of six deliveries.

Progression: Move from a drop feed to a bobble feed. When using a bobble feed, batsmen can be back to back in the nets, but ensure that they are a safe distance apart so there is no danger of them hitting each other with their bats. It is advisable to have some sort of buffer outside the net for the batsman hitting in that direction.

Coaching aim: With less experienced players it is not necessary to be over-specific about whether their drives should be lofted or on the floor. You just want to encourage them to present a full face of the bat and get their hands through the line. Skills are developed through repetition.

Pull shot (see sessions 9, 19)

Set-up and equipment: Three bats-men per net, a safe distance apart and facing either into or out of the net so their shots will be played into the side of the nets. Ensure that batsmen are not hitting towards each other or in dangerous areas where other players might be. Each batsman has a tee placed on top of a stump. Ball on top of the tee.

How it works: After demonstration, batsmen practise playing a pull shot.

Progression: Move from hitting the ball off a tee to an underarm feed that should arrive at the batsman between waist and shoulder height. One option is for the feeder to be on one knee, throwing the ball up to the batsman, replicating the bounce from a short-pitched ball.

Alternative: This can be adapted for the cut shot, the cross-batted shot into the off side.

Coaching aim: It is a cross-batted shot into the leg side and the batsman's hands should come from high to low across the front of his body.

Sweep shot (see session 12)

Set-up and equipment: Batsmen working in pairs (one to feed, one to play the shot); three pairs per net a safe distance apart; batsmen hitting into the side of the net. Soft balls.

How it works: The batsman gets into the 'finish' position where his front knee is flexed 90 degrees and the back knee touches the ground. The feeder delivers a low underarm one-bounce feed for the batsman to play the sweep. He should repeat six times and then swap with his partner.

Progression: The batsmen start in their normal pre-delivery stance and play the shot from start to finish with the same low one-bounce feed.

Coaching aim: The batsman learns to have his weight forward and hands coming from high to low, similar to the pull shot.

BATTING GAMES
Front-foot drive game (see session 6)

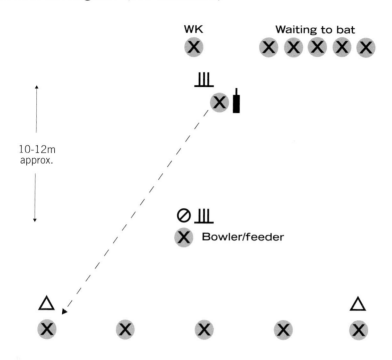

Set-up and equipment: Two teams: one batting, the other fielding. Two sets of stumps 10–12m apart. Two cones or single stumps roughly 3m from either side of the batting stumps. Two cones beyond the feeder's stumps as the designated target area. Vary the width of the area according to ability. Another option is to have two sets of cones, one narrower than the other. Extra points are scored for hitting through the narrower cones. Fielders are placed beyond the cones, other than the wicketkeeper.

How it works: The feeder (having the coach do it ensures a fair and consistent feed) delivers an underarm one-bounce throw to the batsman, who tries to drive the ball between the cones. If the batsman hits the ball between the cones he scores one; if he beats the fielders in the coned area he scores two. Fielders are encouraged to walk in as they would in a match. A batsman faces six balls or until he is caught or bowled out. Fielders rotate clockwise after each set of six balls when a new batsman comes in.

Coaching aim: Straight driving.

Pairs batting (see session 1)

Set-up and equipment: Similar to front-foot drive game (see previous page) but with the group split into pairs. Two sets of stumps. One pair bats, one player bowls, all others field.

How it works: Each batting pair receives 18 deliveries. A batsman must run if he hits it and call for the run before setting off. He loses runs if he does not call. To encourage straight hitting, place two cones about 20m apart behind the bowler. Batsmen score double runs for hitting between the cones. Fielders should have their hands touching the walls of the sports hall and be encouraged to walk in as the bowler bowls. The batsmen receive a free hit (when they cannot be out) if fielders do not walk in. Batsmen lose three runs if they are out. In order to avoid anyone having a negative score, which can be demotivating, it is advisable to give them a starting score of, say, 50 or 100 runs.

Variation: Teams rather than pairs. Batsmen can bat as long as they like but are out when they are out, so start from nought rather than having a bank of runs already. You can retire them after a certain amount of time or number of runs scored.

Coaching aims: Encourage straight hitting; finding the gaps in the field; calling before setting off for a run.

Target batting (see session 12)

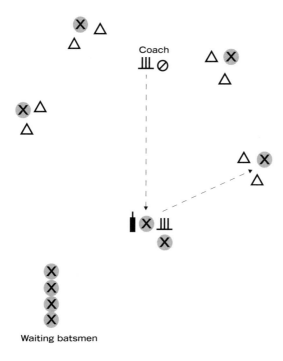

Coach

Waiting batsmen

Set-up and equipment: Two sets of stumps, cones, tennis balls or IncrediBalls®. Two teams, one fielding/collecting balls and the other batting.

How it works: Coach bobble feeds the ball to the batsman having nominated in advance a coloured gate for the ball to be hit through. Score two points for hitting the ball through the correct gate, one point for the wrong gate and zero for not hitting a target.

Progression: This is very easy to vary according to ability. Make the gates bigger or smaller, nearer or further away, as required. Make all the targets carry equal value if that is simpler. Vary the number of balls for each batsman. You can make it even more competitive by ruling that a batsman is out if he misses the designated target.

Coaching aim: Batsmen hitting into the gaps in the field and therefore finding those vital singles to keep the scoreboard ticking over. Hitting straight and driving on both sides of the wicket with good technique: weight moving forward, head over the ball, bat coming through straight.

Soft hands (see session 14)

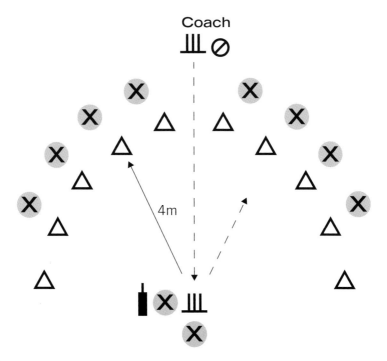

Set-up and equipment: Two sets of stumps. Arc of cones no more than 4m from the batsman. IncrediBalls® (tennis balls will be too bouncy). Six balls per batsman.

How it works: Coach delivers underarm feeds to the batsman who plays a defensive shot at the ball but tries to keep the ball within the arc of cones. Safety must be emphasised, with fielders in close, and the importance of playing a defensive shot.

Progression: Split the group into two teams. The batsman scores a point for his team if he defends his wicket and keeps the ball within the arc of cones. Make it harder by only allowing a point to be scored if he survives six balls. The coach can make it harder for batsmen by adding spin to the ball.

Coaching aim: Playing the ball late with 'soft' hands to hit the ball short of the infield and create the possibility of a quick run, a vital tool in a match situation for rotating the strike and keeping the scoreboard ticking over.

Sweep shot game (see session 12)

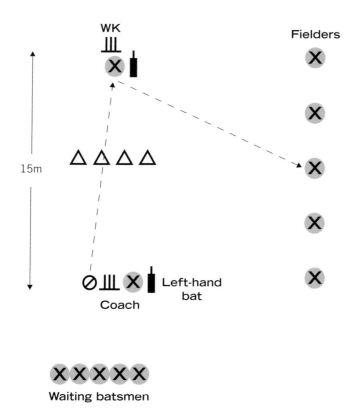

Set-up and equipment: Two sets of stumps; cones; players in two teams, one batting, one fielding. Fielders line up along a notional boundary line. If this is played indoors the stumps should be set up well over to one side of the hall to give enough safe hitting space to the batsman. Soft balls. Waiting batsmen should be well away from the hitting area.

How it works: The coach underarms a two-bounce feed; the batsman plays a sweep shot. The fielders attempt to field the ball and return it to the wicketkeeper. The batsman can score by running to the cones and back or by hitting the ball through the fielders (four or six if it hits the wall/clears boundary on the full). A left-handed batsman should bat at the opposite end, with the coach and keeper swapping ends. Fielders stay where they are. Each batsman receives six balls.

Coaching aims: Focus on the head going down the line of the ball and hands coming from high to low.

Pull shot game

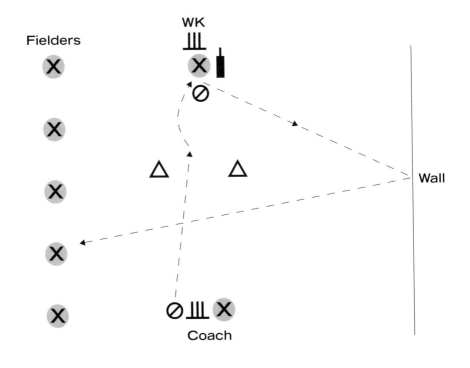

Fielders

WK

Wall

Coach

Waiting batsmen

Set-up and equipment: As for the sweep-shot game, but if played indoors the fielders must be on the off side of the batsman for safety reasons. Make sure too that the balls being used are safe. One option is to use spongy balls rather than tennis balls or Incrediballs®.

How it works: It works in the same way as the sweep game but the fielders gather the ball on the rebound from the wall rather than on the full to ensure safety. You can have them taking the ball on the full if there is enough room and the environment is safe.

Coaching aims: Keep the head still, maintain balance and have the hands come from high to low.

Running between the wickets game (see session 14)

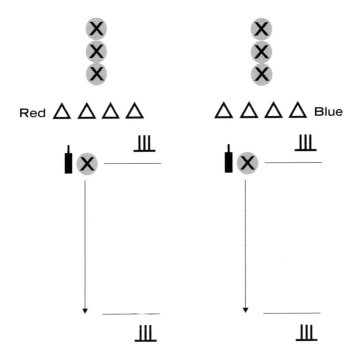

Set-up and equipment: Four sets of stumps; two sets of differently coloured cones. Players split into two groups with bats and gloves. For safety, it is better to have the waiting players well back from the stumps where the racing batsmen will be running to and past. Either have them behind a set of cones or off to the side of the hall or practice area.

How it works: 1. Players simply race against their opposite number (try to pair up players with similar running ability) to the other set of stumps, the winner collecting a point for his team. The coach's command starts each race but the batsmen have to call 'yes' as if calling for a run in a match before they set off. 2. Start to drip-feed information (see pictures on the following page) about running between the wickets, beginning with how to hold the bat; how and when to run it into the crease; that the shortest distance between two points is a straight line, because players often veer off to the side as they approach the stumps. 3. After each piece of information, players race each other. 4. Now they can play an imaginary shot before running a two. The coach calls whether this shot should be off side or leg side, ensuring that the players know the difference. If they do not, now is a good time to explain or remind them. The use of coloured cones aids the distinction between which side the notional ball has been played and also avoids possible confusion for left-handed batsman, for whom leg and off side is the opposite way round. 5. Remind them of/explain the importance of not turning blind, i.e. batsmen need to be facing in the direction where the ball was hit when they are ready to turn for a possible second or third run. This may require a batsman to switch the hand in which he is carrying his bat.

Progression: One team are batsmen, the other become fielders (see digram opposite). The coach drops a ball for a fielder to attack and throws the ball to a player at the stumps where the batsman is heading.

Coaching aim: To learn and practise the fundamentals of running between the wickets: calling, running straight, not turning blind.

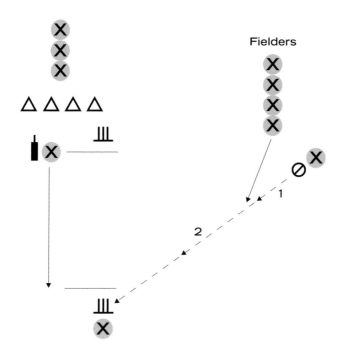

Fielders

Former England captain Michael Vaughan practises running between the wickets.

ECB safety guidance on the wearing of helmets by young players up to the age of 18

Helmets with a faceguard or grille should be worn when batting against a hard cricket ball in matches and in practice sessions. Young players should regard a helmet with a faceguard as a normal item of protective equipment when batting, together with pads, gloves and, for boys, an abdominal protector (box).

Young wicketkeepers should wear a helmet with a faceguard, or a wicketkeeper face protector when standing up to the stumps. With the assistance of schools, cricket clubs and leagues, the wearing of helmets by young players is now standard practice in cricket throughout England and Wales. Helmets are widely available and are covered by a British Standard. A face protector represents an alternative head protection system for young wicketkeepers. Wicketkeeper face protectors are covered by a new British Standard.

This guidance applies to all players up to the age of 18, both in adult cricket and in all junior cricket played with a hard cricket ball. The guidance also applies during all practice sessions. Any individual taking responsibility for players should take all reasonable steps to ensure that this guidance is followed at all times. The ECB asks that the guidance is communicated to the parents or guardians of all young players through clubs and schools, and that young players are not allowed to bat or stand up to the stumps when keeping wicket against a hard ball without wearing appropriate protection.

BOWLING DRILLS # 7.

BASICS AND SAFETY

Bowling can be a complicated business, and as players develop their skills and become more experienced there is great benefit in seeking specialist coaching. This is not just so that players can develop their skills to the maximum, but also to ensure that, biomechanically, their bowling is as sound as possible. Bowlers can sometimes develop what is known as a 'mixed action', when their hips and shoulders are not properly aligned. This can lead to serious injury.

The basic drills that follow focus on the fundamentals of a bowler completing his bowling action and developing the ability to bowl a good line and length. These fundamentals are the foundation of good bowling, whether a bowler is just starting out or opening the bowling in a Test match. Whatever level a bowler has reached, and whatever skills of swing, seam or spin he might have developed, there is still always merit in grooving his action with targets for accuracy of length or guiding markers to assist in the consistent production of that off-stump line.

Coaches should always be mindful of not overworking young bowlers, and the ECB's directives for young fast bowlers appear in this chapter. It is important always that young players feel a sense of achievement from any practice session. Bowling can seem quite daunting to some young cricketers, so it is vital that targets or goals are realistic and achievable according to ability. For example, if you have target areas on the ground for bowlers to land the ball in, make sure they are large enough so that bowlers have a realistic chance to succeed. Players can always be challenged further if they find something too easy, but you do not want a player leaving a session feeling he has not achieved anything. If you are introducing bowling to a group, give them very basic goals such as delivering the ball to their partner so the ball bounces only once or trying to deliver the ball with a straight arm. Another option is to have players go through the basic bowling action with no ball in their hand so they get used to the feeling of bowling with a straight arm. To the experienced cricketer these things will seem very basic but they are important fundamentals that the novice or inexperienced cricketer must achieve in a supportive environment and not be put off.

The coaching aims that accompany the explanations of each drill are examples to aid the coach. They are not necessarily the only technical elements involved in the execution of a particular delivery or skill.

BOWLING DRILLS AND COMPETITIONS
Straight-line bowling (see sessions 3, 5, 13)
Set-up and equipment: Players line up in pairs opposite each other with one ball per pair.

How it works: Players bowl to each other, ideally using the lines in a sports hall or a line of cones to develop a straight-line bowling action.

Progression: How to swing the ball and the importance of shining the ball.

Coaching aims: It is impossible to look at the whole bowling action all of the time, so it is best to isolate certain key aspects to concentrate on, including: 1. Head travelling down the line, 2. Front arm driving forward towards the target, making sure the bowler completes his action, 3. Follow through towards the target by staying on the line, 4. How to grip the ball.

Line and length bowling (see session 7)

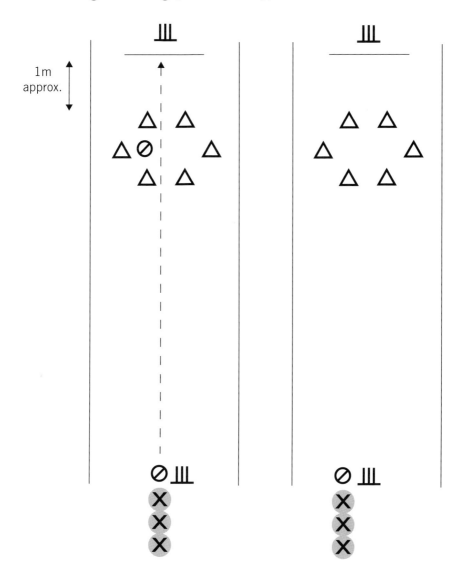

Set-up and equipment: Players each have a ball. A coned-off target set up in the nets on a good length around off stump. The definition of a good length can vary depending on the height and ability of batsmen and bowlers. But you want inexperienced bowlers to learn the importance of bowling a full length, so the cones can be a metre from the batting crease or even closer.

How it works: Players bowl their balls aiming for the target.

Progression: Bowling to a left-hander by adjusting angle of run-up.

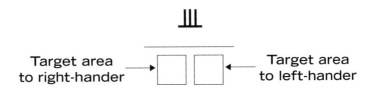

Target area to right-hander → □ □ ← Target area to left-hander

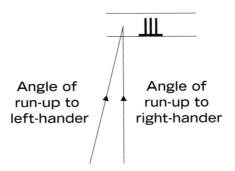

Angle of run-up to left-hander   Angle of run-up to right-hander

Coaching aim: Bowling a full length.

Spin bowling basics (see session 10)

Set-up and equipment: Same principles as straight-line bowling. Players in pairs opposite each other, one ball per pair.

How it works: After demonstrations of basic grips for off-spin and leg-spin, players bowl to their partners, trying to make the ball spin. Ideally each pair should be standing on a sports hall line, or a line of cones and then trying to spin the ball from one side of the line to the other side. To start, players can be encouraged simply to throw the ball with the sole aim of trying to make the ball spin. Then you can progress to a full bowling action. Call players for review and feedback at regular intervals.

Progression: 1. If you have a group where certain players have developed spin-bowling skills they can work separately with another coach or assistant, 2. Players bowl into a net with target areas.

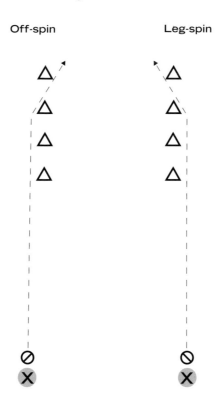

Coaching aim: Understanding the basic grip and trying to spin the ball hard.

Basic grip for an off-spin delivery.

Basic grip for a leg-spin delivery.

Bowling grid under pressure (see session 7)

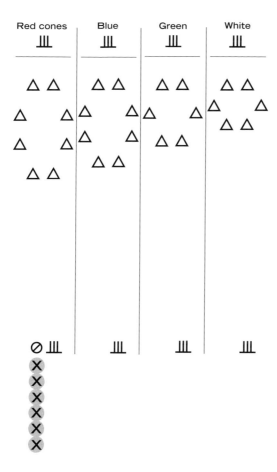

Set-up and equipment: Four sets of stumps lined up in parallel, one pitch-length apart. Then set up a target area with cones (different coloured cones for each target area). These should be positioned on a full length just outside off stump. The size of the targets should vary according to the ability of your players. The first one could be as large as 6m × 4m if required and then diminish gradually. It is important that players go home with a sense of achievement, so ensure the targets are realistic.

How it works: Players start by trying to bowl the ball inside the largest target and then progress to the next, smaller targets once they complete the first one.

Coaching aim: Accuracy under pressure.

Bowling competition (see session 3, 13)

Set-up and equipment: Players split into three or four teams. Two sets of stumps each per team, set up one pitch-length apart. One player is wicketkeeper.

How it works: Players bowl the ball at the stumps and follow the ball through to replace the wicketkeeper. The keeper goes to back of the bowling queue and the next bowler bowls. The winning team is the one that hits the stumps most often in two minutes.

Progression: 1. Remove a stump each time the stumps are hit (ensure these are placed in a safe area). The team who gets all three stumps removed first is the winner, 2. Set up four sets of stumps next to each other so you have a target of 12 stumps. Bowlers bowl from a normal pitch-length's distance away. Each bowler represents their team and tries to score a point by hitting the target. It might seem easy but all their team-mates and the other teams are sitting on the side watching. To add a sense of pressure and extra competition, opposition players are permitted to create some crowd noise or slow hand-clap as the bowler runs in.

Coaching aim: Bowlers to complete their action properly as they would in a game, including a follow-through.

Caught and bowled

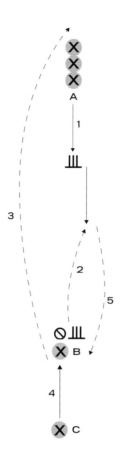

Set-up and equipment: A normal pitch-length with stumps at either end in parallel with each other. In each, one player with a ball acting as wicketkeeper (B) at one set of stumps. Other players line up a decent distance behind the bowler's end stumps (A) to allow each bowler a decent run-up. One player is positioned 10m behind the stumps at C.

How it works: Bowlers run in without a ball and complete their normal bowling action. As they are completing their action, B underarms them a catch. B runs to the back of the queue at A while C runs to the stumps to take a throw from the bowler. C takes the place as keeper while the bowler now moves to position C.

Coaching aim: Bowlers learn to react to a possible catch while in their bowling follow-through, so are possibly off balance or unprepared. Fielders learn to come to the stumps to receive throws for possible run-out opportunities.

Back-foot bowling circuit

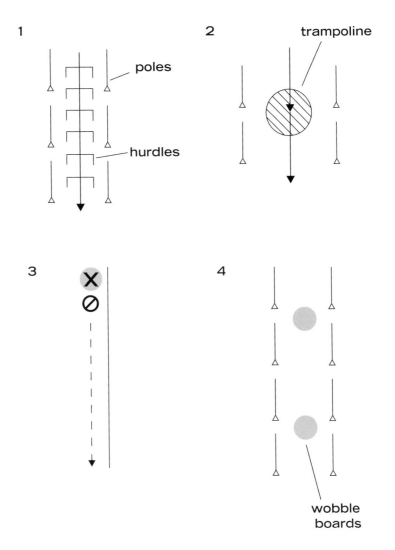

Set-up and equipment: This is for more advanced bowlers and requires equipment that not everyone will have available: six hurdles, 16 poles (or cones), one mini trampoline, two wobble boards. Four stations are set out as follows: 1. Six hurdles no more than 0.5m apart in a straight corridor defined by poles, 2. Mini trampoline in a short corridor defined by poles, 3. Stumps and straight line denoted either by a line in a sports hall or a series of cones to mark a narrow corridor, 4. Two wobble boards in a narrow corridor defined by poles.

How it works: This is a circuit where bowlers take turns on the different stations. On 1 the bowlers set themselves in their normal bowling action as they would be about to deliver the ball and hop using only their back foot over the hurdles, all the while trying to maintain their posture. It is important that their starting position is their normal bowling action, whether that be side on, front on or in between. 2. Bowler sets himself in his action and hops on to the trampoline, landing on his back foot and then off the other side. 3. This is the one station where a ball is used. The bowler comes off a few paces and tries to bowl the ball as straight as possible. 4. The bowler places a foot on either wobble board and attempts to stay balanced while holding his normal bowling action.

Coaching aim: For bowlers to maintain stability and balance.

ECB fast-bowling directives for junior cricketers

Age	Max. overs per spell	Max. overs per day
Up to 13	5	10
U14, U15	6	12
U16, U17, U18, U19	7	18

For the purpose of these directives, a fast bowler is defined as a bowler to whom a wicketkeeper in the same age group would in normal circumstances stand back to take the ball.

Having completed a spell the bowler cannot bowl again, from either end, until the equivalent number of overs to the length of his spell have been bowled from the same end. A bowler can change ends without ending his current spell, provided that he bowls the next over that he legally can from the other end. If this does not happen his spell is deemed to be concluded. If play is interrupted for any reason, for less than 40 minutes, any spell in progress at the time of the interruption can be continued after the interruption up to the maximum number of overs per spell for the appropriate age group.

If the spell is not continued after the interruption the bowler cannot bowl again, from either end, until the equivalent number of overs to the length of his spell before the interruption have been bowled from the same end. If the interruption is of 40 minutes or more, whether scheduled or not, the bowler can commence a new spell immediately.

Once a bowler covered by these directives has bowled in a match he cannot exceed the maximum number overs per day for his age group, even if he subsequently bowls spin. He can exceed the maximum overs per spell if bowling spin, but cannot then revert to bowling fast until an equivalent number of overs to the length of his spell have been bowled from the same end.

If he bowls spin without exceeding the maximum number of overs in a spell the maximum will apply as soon as he reverts to bowling fast. Captains, team managers and umpires are asked to ensure that these directives are followed at all times.

For guidance it is recommended that in any seven-day period a fast bowler should not bowl more than four days, and for a maximum of two days in a row. Age groups are based on the age of the player at midnight on 31 August in the year preceding the current season.

MIDDLE GAMES AND PRACTICES

8.

OUTDOOR MIDDLE PRACTICE

In a perfect world, weather, time and space would allow you to run outdoor practices on a middle wicket on your club's ground from late March/early April and all through the blissful summer evenings.

In the real world, of course, things are a little different. Even with a dry spring the ground will still be soft underfoot, and groundsmen are unlikely to be massively keen on their lovingly tendered 22 yards of turf being scuffed and cut up a week or two before the season starts. An all-weather strip, which many clubs have these days, is a valuable aid to getting some outdoor practice, though you still need to be comfortable that the outfield is dry enough and firm enough underfoot for a safe and meaningful session. If playing on an all-weather pitch, spiked shoes will not be permitted, making it doubly important that your players are not slipping and sliding all over the outfield.

But if you can get to have some practice in the middle outside before the season or at various points during it, your players will gain so much benefit from it as well having a lot of fun. It enables them – and the coach – to experience the game as it is really played, which can be hard to do indoors or during a net session.

Some tips for running a middle practice are:

- Be mindful of time. You do not want one batsman batting the whole evening
- Rotate the fielders to keep them alert
- Set up match scenarios and set fields accordingly
- Have two bowlers operating at the same time, so when one bowler is walking back to his mark the next bowler is running in to deliver the next ball. This helps to keep players focused and avoids the 'dead' time between deliveries

You can incorporate elements from your drills, such as hitting or scoring areas or awarding a free hit to the batsman if the fielders do not keep the ball off the ground when returning it to the bowler.

INDOOR GAMES

If you are unable to conduct a middle session outdoors you can still run a valuable coaching session indoors.

Continuous cricket (see sessions 2, 9)

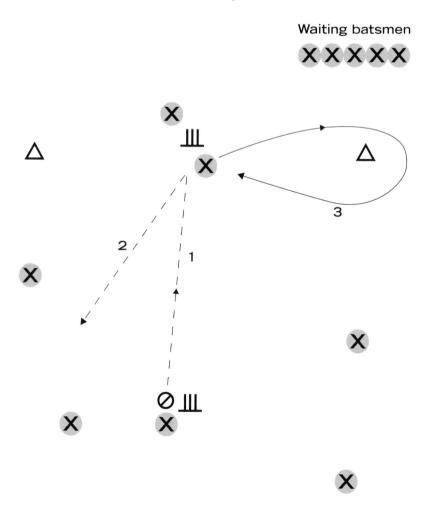

Set-up and equipment: Two teams: one batting, the other fielding. Two sets of stumps 10–12m apart. Two cones or single stumps roughly 3m from either side of the batting stumps.

How it works: The bowler (coach or assistant if necessary) delivers an underarm throw to bounce once to the batsman. Batsmen score four if they hit the back wall on the bounce and six if they hit it on the full. Once they hit the ball they must run round one of the cones near the batting stumps. The ball should be returned to the feeder, who delivers the ball as soon as he receives it. Fielders should be encouraged to walk in. Fielders rotate clockwise after each set of six balls when a new batsman comes in. A batsman should receive a set number of deliveries, say 6 or 12, before being replaced. If he is out he loses five runs. Each batsman should start with a total of runs, 50 for example, so there is no danger of anyone getting a negative score, which can be demoralising. Right-handed batsmen should be encouraged to run to their left (in other words, behind them as they face bowler), so that after running around the cone they arrive back at the stumps in the correct batting position. Left-handers should run around the cone to their right.

Progression: Allow bowlers to bowl overarm. Introduce cones to encourage straight hitting or designated hitting areas where double runs can be scored.

Coaching aim: Teamwork and communication. For fielders, make sure they are walking in.

Tip and run (see sessions 5, 16)

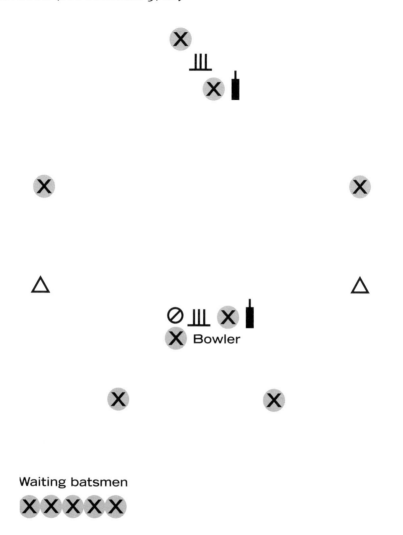

Bowler

Waiting batsmen

Set-up and equipment: Two teams. Two sets of stumps. Two players batting at any one time. Other team-mates waiting to bat. Other team in the field. Two cones positioned to encourage straight hitting.

How it works: Batsmen can bat as long as they like, but initially they will not bat for long as they get used to having to run every time they hit the ball. If they are very good then you can make them retire at a certain score. If a batsman hits between the cones he has a choice whether to run or not (so he is not being penalised for hitting straight). He receives double runs for hitting between the cones. Hitting the back wall is 8 and on the full is 12. Fielders should walk in and batsmen get a free hit if they do not. Fielders should also be encouraged to get into the good habit of keeping the ball off the floor as they return it to the bowler. The batting side receives one run if the fielding side does not keep the ball off the floor. Batsmen can be caught off the side walls if the shot is poor, otherwise award runs accordingly. If there is enough space the waiting batsmen can do keepy-uppy or catching in pairs.

Coaching aims: Batsmen hitting into gaps; calling when running between the wickets.

Sachin Tendulkar plays keepy-uppy with bat and ball.

FIELD SETTINGS 9.

The subtle manoeuvring of fielders by a captain is one of the most intriguing and debated aspects of cricket. The skipper might be forced into plugging holes as an opposition batsman runs amok, or he might be implementing a pre-set plan for a particular bowler or he might have a gut instinct about how a certain batsman is going to play. Moving a fielder from one position to another, only to see a batsman hit a catch straight to him, is one of the most satisfying aspects of the game for a fielding side at any level of the game, and for the coach, who may well have had a direct input into that field change.

Some of the names of cricket's field placings are relatively obvious: square leg is a position square of the wicket on the leg side. Slips, gully or third man are not so obvious. There is no need to dwell on the more obscure derivations of these terms, but it is vital to know where the positions are and why they are there (see also diagrams on pages 130–134). Coaches should be aware of the ECB fielding regulations governing junior cricket and the proximity of close catchers (see page 135).

WHERE THE FIELDERS GO AND WHY
Slips and gully
Where: Catching positions behind the wicket, fanning out from the wicket-keeper, on the off side.

Why: To snaffle those edges from the batsman. Gully will be in line for some thicker edges or more full-blooded shots.

Also: Slips and gully can also be positioned on the leg side for an off-spinner turning the ball sharply into a right-handed batsman or for a left-armer to a left-hander. Or possibly for a left-arm quick bowler to a right-handed batsman if the bowler is swinging the ball into the batsman sharply or the batsman has a tendency to move across his stumps and flick the ball down the leg side. But remember that the laws of the game allow you only two fielders behind square on the leg side.

Third man

Where: Run-saving behind the wicket on the off side, often on or close to the boundary. Can be very fine or straight (i.e. closer to an imaginary line between the two sets of stumps) if there is only one slip (or none) in place. Or wider if the batsman's shot-making determines it.

Why: To stop a thick edge from an attacking shot that might shoot through the slips area or possibly a deliberately guided shot like a late cut.

Point

Where: Square of the wicket on the off side.

Why: A basic run-saving position, most often trying to cut off one run from a dab or push from the batsman, or possibly a full-blooded cut shot.

Also: Can be positioned backward of square, not as close to the batsman as gully, or in a deep position on the boundary square or behind square.

Cover or cover point

Where: Run-saving position a bit straighter (nearer to the bowler) than point.

Why: A key position and one for your top fielder. It is vital for cover to walk in, prowling like a cheetah ready to pounce on the ball or tear after it to the boundary.

Also: Extra cover a bit straighter still. Also deep cover or deep extra cover, on the boundary and often known these days as a sweeper.

Mid-off and mid-on

Where: Behind the bowler to his left and right, they would make a V shape with the batsman as the point of the V.

Why: Standard run-saving positions to stop the off- or on-drives from the batsman. They should be closer for a less attacking batsman and slightly further back for a more aggressive one. A good position for a captain to field because he can liaise easily with his bowler.

Also: Long-off and long-on are the boundary versions of mid-off and mid-on, used when a batsman is hitting out. Look out for those sky-high catches. Silly mid-off and silly mid-on are the opposite: catching positions in front of the batsman. Be aware of the ECB fielding regulations. One for the braver players.

Midwicket

Where: The leg-side equivalent of extra cover.

Why: Not a must-have position but would be standard if you have four or more fielders on the leg side.

Also: Deep midwicket on the boundary. A very useful position to give protection to spin bowlers or when the batsmen are hitting out. Indeed it is a key position at junior level when batsmen tend to try to smash the ball across the leg side rather than hit straight. Young bowlers, who are also learning how to control their length, can benefit from the protection of a deep midwicket.

Square leg

Where: Square of the wicket on the leg side.

Why: A standard run-saving position that can be moved in front or behind square depending on how the batsman is playing or the pace of the pitch. Square leg needs to be prowling like the man at cover but also ready for a stinging catch from a pull shot.

Also: Backward square leg, short square leg (catching) and deep square leg on the boundary.

Fine leg or long leg

Where: The leg-side equivalent of third man.

Why: Normally a boundary fielder (often the fast bowler operating from that end of the ground) to save the leg glances/flicks from the batsman, and also the fine deflections off the batsman's pads (leg byes) that come off the quicker bowlers. Also to save any balls that the wicketkeeper is unable to stop. And he should be ready for those catches that can fly off the edge of the bat when a batsman mistimes a pull or a hook.

Also: Short fine leg, slightly finer/straighter than backward square leg. Often used for a spin bowler.

LEFT-HANDED AND RIGHT-HANDED BATSMEN

A key thing for players to learn and adapt to is how the field needs to change when a right-hand batsman is batting with a left-hander. It is a waste of time and energy for the entire field to cross over (e.g. cover point for the right-hander). The basic field for a right-hander needs very little adaptation, with potentially only slip actually moving across from one side to the other. The other settings can simply shift ever so slightly (e.g. cover point and square leg), or indeed remain in exactly the same position (e.g. mid-off and mid-on). Ideally all your players are so switched on all the time that they do not need to be told when the right-hand/left-hand combination is changing. But even in senior cricket people still need reminding, so it is advisable that either the captain, wicketkeeper or another nominated player alerts their team-mates to a change-over or if a left-handed batsman comes in at the fall of a wicket. A simple call of 'left-hand' or 'right-hand' does the job.

The same applies to the change of ends after each over. It is pointless for mid-on to run to mid-on at the other end after each over, or worse, long-on to long-on, especially if they are bowlers who need to conserve energy. This requires a bit of understanding and alertness to work out that mid-on can become cover point, for example. There are exceptions, of course, because you might always want certain fielders in certain positions.

Example field-setting for a right-arm pace bowler to a right-hand batsman

OFFSIDE   LEGSIDE

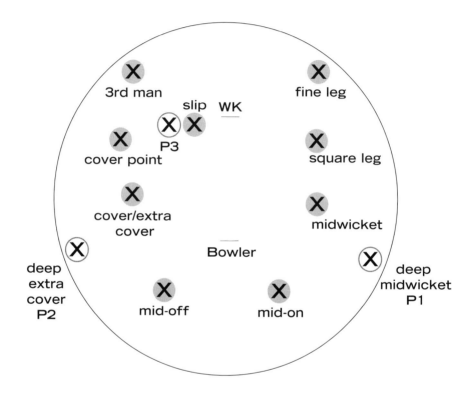

This is a basic split field with five men on the off side and four on the leg. If a bowler is able to bowl a consistent line on off stump then you can adapt it accordingly.

Adaptation: Player at midwicket could move deeper (P1) if the batsman is hitting through the infield on the leg side. Or if the bowler is bowling a consistent off-stump line but is being hit through the off side you could bring him over to deep extra cover (P2). If the bowler is particularly accurate or swinging it then you could introduce an extra slip or a gully (P3).

Example field-setting for a right-arm off-spin bowler to a right-hand batsman

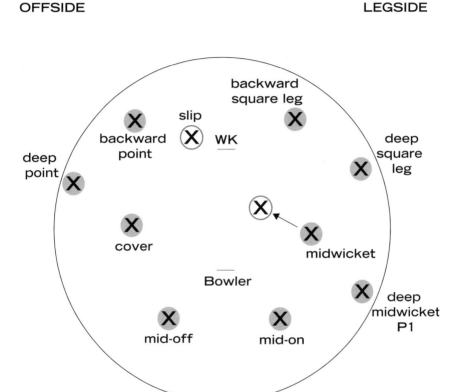

OFFSIDE   LEGSIDE

Two men on the leg-side boundaries give a young off-spinner the protection he needs, whether he is spinning the ball (into the right-hander) or not. He is likely to drop the odd ball short so the deep point gives him protection on the off side. The mid-off and mid-on should be up, saving the single, to entice the batsman to hit over the top. You have to be a very good player to do that.

Adaptation: Things change if he starts bowling well or is more experienced. You can be more attacking by bringing deep point (also known as a sweeper) into slip. You can also bring midwicket into a catching position at short mid-wicket/silly mid-on but you must ensure that the catcher is wearing a helmet and complies with the ECB fielding regulations for junior cricket (see panel on page 135). It is not nice for a batsman to see a catcher in his field of vision. If you are a very accurate or experienced spinner you might bowl four 'dots' in the over then move mid-on back towards the boundary (long-on). The batsman has an easy single but he has been tied down so he might try to hit out and be caught.

Example field-setting for a right-arm leg-spin bowler or left-arm spinner to a right-hand batsman

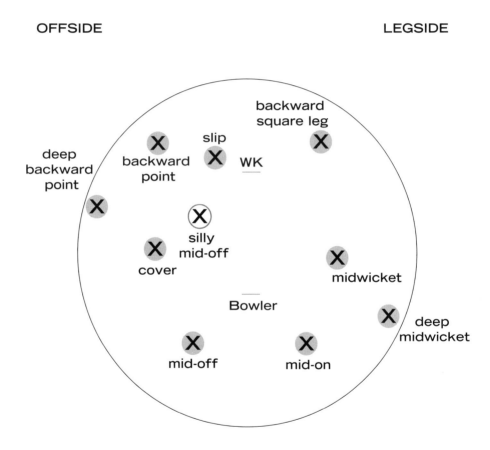

OFFSIDE   LEGSIDE

Any young leg-spinner needs some protection, particularly deep on the leg side. They are likely to drop short on the off side, hence the deep cover point (sweeper). The slip gives him some encouragement, especially if he is spinning the ball.

The left-arm spinner is less likely to drop short, so there might be an opportunity for an extra catcher on the off side (deep backward point to silly mid-off).

Example field-setting for a left-arm pace bowler to a right-hand batsman

OFFSIDE   LEGSIDE

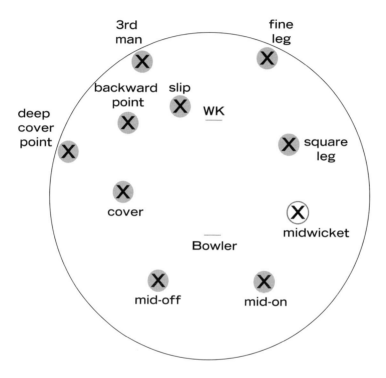

For the left-armer you would typically have square-leg more in front of square than with a right-armer. The fine leg is there if the bowler loses his line and goes down the leg side.

Adaptation: If the bowler is swinging the ball into the right-handed batsman then you will require an extra man on the leg side. If he is swinging it away, working with the natural angle across the batsman, then you can look at an extra catcher on the off side at slip or gully.

Example field-setting for a right-arm pace bowler to a right-hand batsman at the end of an innings

OFFSIDE

LEGSIDE

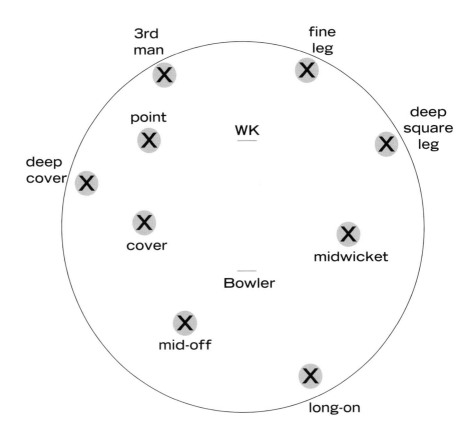

The bowler is trying to bowl full and straight. Mid-off is up on the basis that few junior cricketers would be able to hit over the top in that area. At a higher standard this might not necessarily be the case. Long-on might need to be moved wider towards deep midwicket, depending on the ability of the batsman and the accuracy of the bowler.

FIELD SETTINGS GAME

And now to teach your players where the field settings are. This is a good rainy day/evening option or can form part of a winter session. But there needs to be some activity or competition element to it because players will not react well to feeling they are back in the classroom. You can give the players information about field settings to go away with and have a look at it in anticipation of an activity focusing on it the following week.

Set-up and equipment: Create a mini cricket field and mark out all the standard field settings using flat discs that can be written on. Lay out the discs on the sports hall floor, making sure that wicketkeeper and bowling positions can be clearly marked.

How it works: If your players have little or no knowledge of fielding settings then the first thing to do is to talk through where the positions are and what their names are. One option is to have given them a sheet illustrating the fielding positions the week before to digest. Then start to develop their knowledge by naming a target position and asking them to walk or jog to that position. Because this is a relatively static, learning-based activity, it can be a good idea to combine it with dynamic stretching or SAQ to make it more fun. For example, introduce a ladder or hurdles before the players enter the mini field. Or suggest a type of stretch to be done, such as 'lunges to mid-off' or 'sumos to fine leg'. Even turn it into a whole SAQ circuit. Once the players have become reasonably familiar with the fielding positions, collect up the discs (but leaving the markings for wicketkeeper and bowler) and split the players into two teams. Each player takes it in turn to place a disc (that has a fielding position written on it) in the correct place. If they get it right they score a point for their team. If players are more experienced or knowledgeable then go straight into the team competition. This can also be turned into a great activity for a summer practice on a rainy day by using a white board to illustrate the field placings.

Progression: Challenge more experienced players, who have some tactical awareness, to recall whole field settings for certain bowlers or certain types of match situations.

ECB fielding regulations for junior cricket

The ECB has regulations covering the minimum fielding distances for young players in all matches where a hard ball is used:

- No young player in the Under 15 age group or younger shall be allowed to field closer than 8 yards (7.3 metres) from the middle stump, except behind the wicket on the off side, until the batsman has played at the ball.
- For players in the Under 13 age group and below the distance is 11 yards (10 metres).
- These minimum distances apply even if the player is wearing a helmet.
- Should a young player in these age groups come within the restricted distance the umpire must stop the game immediately and instruct the fielder to move back.
- In addition any young player in the Under 16 to Under 18 age groups, who has not reached the age of 18, must wear a helmet and, for boys, an abdominal protector (box) when fielding within 6 yards (5.5 metres) of the bat, except behind the wicket on the off side. Players should wear appropriate protective equipment whenever they are fielding in a position where they feel at risk.
- Age groups are based on the age of the player at midnight on 31 August in the year preceding the current season.

MATCH-DAY MANAGEMENT

10.

PREPARATION AND SELECTION

The first thing to remember is that the match does not start when the first ball is bowled. As with every other aspect of coaching, the better you prepare the better your chances of success on the day. Look at your fixtures well in advance of the season getting under way and start to highlight any potential problem dates, such as school holiday times when players might be away or even situations like a big football match in a major tournament that kids (and parents) might want to watch on TV. You hope that they are committed to your team but you have to be pragmatic about these things. Forewarned is forearmed.

You should try to get your players' availability as early as possible and certainly urge them to flag up definite periods of unavailability, such as family holidays, in good time. And with most young players the issue of availability will ultimately be the responsibility of the players' parents, so it is vital that communication lines are always open and both parties realise the importance of clarity when it comes to availability rather than offering 'if's and 'maybe's. Few things have the potential to cause stress and upset as much as the thorny issue of selection. It is impossible to keep everyone happy all the time but that does not mean you should not try. Ultimately playing cricket should be a fun, enjoyable experience, so you need to be honest, fair and diplomatic.

It is inevitable that you will have a range of abilities in your group, and there are many factors that will go into deciding how you pick your side or sides. One option is to have the more talented players playing above their age group. Not only does this mean that they are being challenged, but it also relieves that awkward tension where better players feel they are too good for a team. This may not work for everyone, and you have to be mindful of the wishes of the player and the parents. They may need some persuading that this is the best policy. For example, a player may be worried that he will not be playing with his friend. In which case, look to move two or three players into the older age group.

If you have more than one team in an age group then one selection option is to run them in parallel. In other words, do not pick an A, B and C team, in the traditional sense, but spread your talent equally across the teams and give them names like Spitfires or Trojans. This gives other players the opportunity to play alongside the best players and it also means the club can easily defend its selection policy. When the question of why Jimmy is in the A team arises, you can explain that the talent is spread across the various teams. If there are personality clashes or certain players want to play with their mates then, within reason, this can be accommodated.

If someone has paid to be part of a cricket club then you have a duty to give them the chance to play competitive cricket whatever their level of ability. There's no point in picking the same XI just to win every match. You need to give people opportunities. This needs to be stated up front and parents need to understand and buy into it. If you play in a league and a cup competition you could use the cup competition to pick your best sides while spreading the talent or rotating a squad in the league.

HOW TO SELECT A CAPTAIN

You often find that certain players almost inherit the captaincy of a team from a very young age, perhaps because they have started playing very young and their father is an experienced and knowledgeable player. It is nice, though, to be able to empower your players and give different players this opportunity. As you go through your winter net sessions, you should always encourage feedback and questions about the game, discuss tactics so hopefully one or two captaincy candidates will emerge over that time. In a club side, the vagaries of player availability will almost certainly mean that it will be impractical to have the same captain for every game. The cliché about having 11 captains is right: in a perfect world all of your players will be thinking about the game in the same way that the captain has to. The ideal is to help everyone understand the laws of the game, tactics, field placings and how to win.

MATCH-DAY ESSENTIALS

If you are the home team there are various things that you need to be responsible for. You must ensure that there are drinks and refreshments for the opposition; that the toilet facilities are clean and accessible; and also that you have access to a first-aid kit should there be any injuries. Obviously you will need cricket balls, stumps and bails. You will need a scorebook of some sort and a scoreboard that is visible and can be kept updated through the game.

Ideally your club's bar will be open so there is the opportunity for the club to make some money from match evenings. Encourage the parents to come along and watch and have a drink. You can extend that principle and run a barbeque to make an evening of it. If a parent has been watching their child play cricket all evening with a likely finish at around 9 p.m., the last thing they want to do is have to cook an evening meal. The additional benefit of this is to create a buzz around the club and reinforce the bond between parents and players and the club. You do not want kids simply to play a few games for the club and then move on to other things. Ideally you want them to become passionate and dedicated club members for life!

GAME TIME

The length of matches will vary according to standard and age group, but for the moment let us assume that you have a 20-overs-per-side match starting at 6 p.m. on a weekday evening. Players should always look the part at the very least. And a big part of that is warming up and preparing properly for a match. Try to insist that the warm-up starts at 5.30 p.m. That means that the players are changed and good to go as a group at that point, not turning up then. This is the ideal scenario; time constraints may make this impossible but that should be the aspiration.

You can tell a lot by the way a team warms up. One side warms up properly, having got there nice and early. The other team turns up a bit late, maybe there is one dad hitting some balls, then one ball gets lost under a bush and it all looks a bit shambolic. Make sure your team is the first one.

Preparation is something players control and so can you as the coach. If your opening bowler lands the first ball in the right area because he is properly warmed up and has already bowled some practice balls, that is miles better than sending a ball for four wides down the leg side because he has just come straight from school.

WARM-UP DRILLS

How much you can do, of course, depends on time. There may be players who come from quite a distance while others are close by. So you have to tailor your drills accordingly, but the aim is to get a good clear half-hour of warm-ups before the match. However much time you have, intensity is the key: catching 20 balls in three minutes is much better than catching 30 balls in half an hour. Go straight into an organised activity (see chapter 5 'Warm-up and fielding drills') to get the guys running around together as a group, and also making a bit of noise. Next, do some dynamic stretching exercises: that means stretching on the move in small groups, replicating the sort of stretches they will be required to make during the game.

Then there are fielding drills (see chapter 5 'Warm-up and fielding drills'). Ideally you will have one or two other volunteers to assist, in which case you can have a number of different fielding stations: a 'nick off' station for the wicketkeeper and close fielders to practise catching the edges; high catches, short catches and throwing at the stumps. The key thing is lots of repetition. If you are on your own then the drills will require quite a bit of running from one station to another.

The bowlers and batsmen should warm up as if they are in a match situation. If a bowler is going to bowl 20 balls in the match then have him bowl 20 balls in the warm-up, if there is time. They should bowl off their proper run-ups. Set up one set of stumps with cones placed on the various lengths of delivery that they will aim for during a game. Have them aim for a good length and then go for yorkers to replicate the end of an innings. Replicate different phases of the game as opposed to just running up and bowling with no specific purpose. Of course, not all bowlers are able to deliver the ball to order, so only take these warm-up drills to this level of detail if the bowlers are capable of achieving it and have practised it before.

But the important point is that there should be a purpose to their warm-ups. Bowlers should not simply run up and bowl aimlessly. Likewise, batsmen should play proper shots that they will use in the match. Do not allow batsmen simply to slog aimlessly at the ball.

THE TOSS

It is a good idea to get the coin toss done nice and early so that you can prepare for what you are doing. If your team is bowling first then that is the time to make sure the guys get changed, if they are not already. If your team is batting then there is no real point in your bowlers carrying on bowling in the nets.

You will have chosen a captain and hopefully you will have an understanding of how much experience and game sense he has. It is important to empower the captain regardless of how much experience he has. The first thing is to ask him what he thinks and what he thinks of the pitch. It should ultimately be his decision whether to bat or bowl first, but you can ensure that he has taken into consideration things such the possibility of fading light in the latter stages of the game. Batting first is often easier because junior cricketers can freeze in a run chase. Even if you are defending a small total like 80, it can become very hard for the opposition if you take one or two early wickets. Another factor in favour of batting first is that when you play away games there's a chance that some of your team members might arrive late, and you do not want to be going out to field in that situation so you would choose to bat first.

UMPIRING

You are in a very fortunate situation if you do not also have to umpire the matches that you are managing or coaching. Most clubs do not have that luxury, so the likelihood is you will have to umpire the games. Having the two opposing coaches/managers officiating can become a contentious issue. If your side is batting you will be standing alongside one of your side's batsmen when you are umpiring at the bowler's end. There will be a strong temptation to talk to your player and offer observations. It is also common for the fielding side's umpire to make suggestions about moving the field.

You need to create an understanding up front with your opposite number about what the purpose of the match is and what the rules of engagement are. You might legitimately feel that your role is to develop and improve players, in which case talking to them freely without taking too much time out of the game is all right. If you feel that trust might be abused then agree with your opposite number that you will both keep quiet and let the players get on with it. It is vital to establish these ground rules before the first ball is bowled, in order to ensure the game is played in a good spirit.

You also need to establish up front what your ruling on wides will be. Ideally anything down the leg side would be called 'wide', but that is tough on guys who might not have played a huge amount of cricket. One possibility is to have markings on the crease either side of the stumps that indicate the parameters for wides. All you are hoping for is some level of consistency, so an honest discussion with the opposing coach is vital.

In an ideal world you would have a scorer, but the likelihood is you will have to do that as well. There are a number of smaller, more portable scorebooks around and increasingly technological innovations, like the CricHQ app, which allows you to score the match on your smart phone. It is helpful to shout out the score at the end of each over.

TACTICS – BATTING
Scoring options

Remind your openers and top-order batsmen about looking to play straight early on and not being loose outside off stump. Suggest to your batsmen that they try to evaluate quickly how the opposition set their fields. Is their inner ring of fielders perhaps set too deep? If so, then it is very easy to pick up runs by playing with soft hands (see chapter 6 'Batting drills and games') and dropping the ball almost by your feet. As long as there is good understanding with your batting partner, it is possible to rotate the strike with singles almost every ball. If the fielders are in really close and singles are hard to come by then batsmen need to explore other ways of scoring.

Hopefully over the winter months batsmen have developed an understanding of where the best scoring areas might be. So now is a good time for them to remind themselves and be encouraged to be positive – with a controlled hit rather than a hopeful slog – when the ball is in their area. In a run-chase it is vital to try and make some contact with the ball so there is at least the chance to score. Remind your batsmen to play proper cricket shots, to play straight and the importance of leaving wickets in hand.

Running between the wickets

Calling needs to be crystal clear. Players need to have trust in their batting partners and to ensure they are backing up at all times. Run the first run very hard each time to put pressure on the opposition and always be ready to look for a second run, even if you ultimately decide not to attempt it. That means a batsman being almost a third of the way back down the pitch after completing the first run, ready to take advantage of any misfield.

The batsmen in the pavilion

At the start of an innings the top four batsmen should be padded up. The openers, of course, are ready to go out to bat and the next man in must be fully prepared. The No. 4 should be padded up but does not need to have his helmet and gloves on. It is probably advisable too for the No. 5 to have his thigh pad on and his pads and gloves next to him, because you do not want batsmen to be scrambling around trying to get ready. However, what is to be discouraged is for batsmen further down the order to be padding up too early. It is not uncommon to see this, and it might be because they just like to be ready, they are keen, or maybe they are trying to make a point that they should be batting higher in the order. But it gives a bad impression to the batsmen out on the pitch if they see the No. 8, for example, getting ready before a wicket has even fallen. The rule of thumb is that there should be two batsmen padded up in the pavilion at any one time. So when the first wicket falls the No. 5 batsman gets ready, and so on.

Players should be encouraged to sit together as a team while they are waiting to bat, even to the point of setting out enough chairs at the start of an innings so that everyone has their spot. It is not good to have players here, there and everywhere. Some might be messing about throwing balls around; maybe one or two are off the other side of the field with their parents who have come to watch. It is a team game and the players should be supporting their mates who are batting and, if they have not yet batted, they should be observing the play and absorbing information that might be useful when it is their turn to bat.

Of course, batsmen like to have felt bat on ball before they go out to bat in a match, but ideally they will have had that opportunity before the match or between innings. It is preferable not to have batsmen disappearing to the nets while the innings is in progress, but any batting practice that does take place during a match situation must be done safely and sensibly. There is no benefit to players giving batsmen throw-downs on the outfield or off the field entirely if the ball is going to deviate hugely. That does nothing for a batsman's confidence. A low full toss or maybe a bobble feed will suffice. And the batsman should simply be looking to make clean contact, not to smash it across the other side of the pitch. Ideally, the tail-end batsmen would feed the balls to the top-order batsmen.

When a batsman is out he will be disappointed, whether he is a novice or someone with 100 Test caps. It is undoubtedly a test of character, but players need to learn that this is part of the game. He must respect the umpire's decision regardless of whether he thinks it is correct or not. This is a non-negotiable part of playing the game in the right spirit. It should be expected that a dismissed batsman sits with his team-mates and supports the other batsmen once he has taken off his kit. There should be no room for petulance or histrionics, and even if the coach is umpiring he should still be able to communicate to his players on the side. Players also need to learn the responsibilities of supporting their team-mate who has just got out, maybe for a low score or in a tight situation.

TACTICS – BOWLING AND FIELDING

Keep it simple for the bowlers, and as with practice sessions always check for understanding. It is far better for the players to answer a question than simply be told what to do.

It is unreasonable to expect young bowlers to be nailing the right line and length straight away and doing it consistently. But that does not mean they should not try to hit a full length on or outside off stump. You do not want a bowler running up and just putting it anywhere with a field setting that is all over the place. Have a wall of your three best fielders in a ring on the off side. Then get your players thinking about field placings by asking them what happens if the ball gets through that ring. Depending on how much experience your captain has, it is almost inevitable that tactical discussion will be coach-led, at least to begin with (see chapter 9 'Field settings').

Discuss the importance of starting well and also body language. Positive body language is important and can set the tone, but it is vital that the state of the game does not dictate body language. It is easy to look enthused when the opposition are 20 for five. It is much harder – and much more important – to keep energy levels high and maintain positivity if things are not going so well. One wicket or a few dot balls can change a game. Your bowlers should bowl as many balls as they can to a new batsman, even to a point where you might give the well-set batsman a single so you can get the new batsman on strike.

Set the fielders a challenge to win every ball: if the ball goes through to the keeper without scoring then they have won that ball. These little games within the game can really help to keep concentration and focus, as well as develop enthusiasm for a vital part of the game that so often gets overlooked. You could have a little competition in which each fielder says, 'Right, this is my area and the guy's not going to beat me'. You could make it a little contest between the off-side fielders and leg-side fielders and discuss at the end how they think they did. Do not make it too serious, but it is vital to try to keep everyone in the game all the time.

COACHING BETWEEN INNINGS

You hope that your players will have observed their opponents through the first innings of a match so that in the break between innings you can all discuss the state of the game and how your own team's performance can better that of their opponents. If you can get them thinking about it and coming back with answers then that is a major battle won. Coaching is about you helping players to think for themselves and working out the solutions to problems. It's not about tell, tell, tell.

If your team is batting second, the points of discussion might include how the pitch played. If the ball kept low, for example, then batsmen should be looking to get forward. Discuss how the opposition looked to score their runs – did they work the ball around, picking up singles, or did they try to hit boundaries? Which tactic was more successful? If playing away from home, discuss whether there are aspects to the ground that should be taken into consideration, such as a short boundary on one side or the speed of the outfield. If the outfield is slow, maybe because of long grass, or if the boundaries are quite deep, then your batsmen will need to be prepared to run plenty of twos and threes as boundary shots will be in short supply. If a boundary is particularly short, fielders saving the single may compensate by standing deeper than usual because they are concerned about stopping a four. If this is the case then there may be the opportunity to steal quick singles by playing the ball with soft hands.

If your team is bowling second, it is important to make time to do a proper warm-up before your team goes out to field. You will often see teams do an extensive and enthusiastic warm-up before a match but in between innings tuck into a nice cream tea and not be so well-prepared to bowl after the interval. Do not deprive the players of their tea, of course, but there should be plenty of time to get them out on the field ten minutes before the start for a decent warm-up. It would be very useful to have a parent to help you so that you can have more than one activity going on at the same time. The bowlers can bowl in the nets while the other fielders can do a warm-up drill.

TEAM SPIRIT

Make sure your players look like a cricket team. The skipper should lead them out as a unit, rather than them taking the field in dribs and drabs. Shirts should be tucked in and laces done up. If they are wearing caps they should ideally all be wearing the same caps. These might seem like minor details but they all add up to a greater whole and relate to taking pride in your performance.

Human nature dictates that people will criticise each other when things go wrong, but you must actively discourage it. Your job is to be a custodian of the game and to make sure you leave the game in a better state than when you found it. Come down hard on your players if they abuse each other or the opposition. This is not to say they should not play hard. You want players to try their absolute hardest, and when in the field you want them to be totally focused, with intensity, on every single delivery, doing everything they can to 'win' each ball for their team. One way to maintain players' focus and intensity is to give different players the responsibility for geeing up the rest of the fielders during a specified period, a five-over spell for example. While expecting players to play as hard as possible they must also learn to be accepting of other players who perhaps have different or lesser abilities.

There will be situations where you might have a talented player or players whose personalities do not fit easily into the team ethic. They might put other players down or be confrontational and self-centred. One option is to take players out of their comfort zone – if a young player is very gifted he could play in an upper age group.

But if that is not an option, or at least not immediately, you have to find a way of dealing with this player and creating or re-creating some harmony within the team. Remind that player how he can contribute to the team, how other people perceive him and discuss how he wants to perceived by the others. Does he want his team-mates to resent him? Or does he want them to tell their mates what a great player he is and how much they enjoy being in the same team as him?

AFTER THE GAME

A debrief is essential, regardless of the result. If your team has won then they will be on a high, although some players might not be as happy if they feel they have not contributed a great deal. It is important to bring all your players together as a group because you probably will not see them for another week, or some may not be available the following week. This is the time to get them to reflect on how they have performed and to give them some encouragement. Discuss plans for where they can go from here.

Defeat is coming. It will happen. You have to find ways of picking your players up as best you can. After a while it does not hurt so much. You might want to say to the players that, whatever has happened today, we will walk out of the changing room as proud players. We will thank the opposition and shake their hands, shake the umpires' hands. And the players should also thank each other. Shaking the hands of the opposition is non-negotiable. You don't walk off in another direction; even if you have been badly beaten you need to look them in the eye.

Players should look and act the part, and that includes the pre- and post-match pleasantries. These are very important. You have to uphold the spirit of the game. That is the message, and you hope it is one that they will carry with them for the rest of their lives.

THE FUTURE FOR YOU AND YOUR PLAYERS

11.

THE PLAYERS

As they get older, players need to start taking more responsibility for their own actions as they progress towards playing senior cricket. These key responsibilities include turning up on time, with the right kit, knowing which team they are playing in, what their role in the team is on any given day, and ensuring that they can give future availability information when asked by the coach or manager rather than having to defer to a parent.

Deciding on the right time to introduce a young player to senior cricket is not an exact science. Sometimes it will be obvious and to some extent self-determined. No player should be forced to make a step up, for example to help out a team that is short of players. The better and more physically mature players will most likely have a natural inclination to want to play senior cricket. It is vital for you as the junior coach to liaise with the captain or manager of the senior team to ensure that your player is made to feel welcome and is not put in any uncomfortable situations on or off the field.

It may be that you play yourself and therefore you may get the opportunity to play with some of your players, which will provide an excellent viewpoint from which to judge their progress and appetite for playing in an adult environment. If this is not the case it is best to double-check that the senior captain is aware of the various safety issues regarding the wearing of helmets, fielding restrictions and, if the player is a bowler, the ECB guidelines on the number of overs a young player is permitted to bowl.

When you next see your player it would be advisable to ask for feedback about his experience. Hopefully it will have been a positive one for both parties, but you need to know of any concerns or problems resulting from his step-up at the earliest possible moment.

As players get to 15 or 16 years old there does tend to be a substantial drop-off in participation. It is an issue for every club and there is no denying it is a massive challenge to try to retain all these excellent young players that you have developed and encouraged over the past few years. Youngsters in their mid-teens do become exposed to a range of other interests, and also their schoolwork becomes that much more intense. Cricket requires a greater time commitment than most other sports and not all teenagers find that they are prepared to make that commitment.

Human nature dictates that people, especially youngsters, want to do something that they are good at or derive satisfaction from. This is why the integration of younger players into the senior echelons of the club is such an important, and ultimately rewarding, aspect of the junior coach's role. Your club does not have to have a huge range of senior teams to be able to absorb youngsters into the senior set-up. Even a small club with, say, two Saturday XIs and one or two Sunday sides is perfectly capable of giving good opportunities to youngsters. With an increased focus on the competitiveness of league cricket, Sunday friendlies, with a few wise, older heads and a smattering of enthusiastic youngsters, make a perfect introduction for the junior player. And if youngsters can be selected in pairs or small groups then so much the better, as they immediately have a friendly face in the team.

One factor that can determine the retention of younger players is how sociable your club is. If the cricket club can be a social hub for young and old then even young players whose interest in participation is starting to wane may still be a part of the club because it is somewhere they can still come and socialise with their friends, many of whom may still be playing regularly. If they can retain a connection with and an interest in the club then there is every chance that they will once again become an active player.

Coaching is also a great opportunity for the more mature young players in their late teens. Not only does this provide the club with a burgeoning network of coaching support but it also provides the players with a pathway to continue their involvement in the game as well as giving something back. Players can develop a great sense of self-worth and fulfilment by getting involved in coaching. Being mentored by a player who the youngsters have seen around their club and looked up to also brings another dynamic to their cricketing development.The ECB runs a Young Leaders award and more information can be found on the Development>Coach Education section of their website (www. ecb.co.uk).

THE COACH

It may be that you have already attended an ECB Level 1 coaching course or the equivalent in your country. If not, this is an excellent way to develop and increase your understanding of coaching. In the ECB's own words:

> The Level 1 course is aimed at beginner coaches who will be able to 'assist more qualified coaches, delivering aspects of coaching sessions, normally under direct supervision'. This role may include running warm-ups, cool-downs, small-sided games and small group work. The course is essentially designed for parents and volunteers starting on the coaching pathway.
>
> The course will help coaches prepare for, deliver and review cricket coaching sessions. It will enable them to:
>
> * introduce and develop the game of cricket to people of all ages in a safe and enjoyable way
> * develop and improve players (as people as well as cricketers)
> * develop coaching skills, knowledge and qualities
> * demonstrate competence against UKCC/National standards for coaches
>
> The programme consists of four 3-hour modules and a final assessment.

Having achieved a Level 1 qualification a coach will have the opportunity to join the ECB Coaches Association, which offers a number of benefits including insurance. For more information go to the ECB website: www.ecb.co.uk/development/ecb-coaches-association. The holder of a Level 2 qualification (Coach Award) will be able to 'prepare for, deliver and review coaching sessions'. Level 3, the Performance Coach Course, is aimed at coaches developing players at elite level.

Without volunteer coaches, cricket clubs could not operate successfully and offer such great opportunities to young players. Do not view your role in isolation, as simply coach of the Under 13s, for example. You form part of a club's coaching network, which hopefully can be a steadily growing pyramid under the auspices of a junior coaching coordinator. Every club is different, of course, and there is no point in growing your player base enthusiastically if you do not have the facilities or the coaching resources to handle it. A player who comes to a chaotic session with too many kids involved will not come back in a hurry. But with good communication, enthusiasm and dedication you can contribute so much, not just to a player or a team but to the overall health of your club, school or community. This is not just about coaching cricketers or trying to help a team win matches. It is as much about developing young people with an appreciation of the importance of teamwork, of dealing with success and failure. Cricket offers so many lessons in life that can be communicated effectively by a dedicated and enthusiastic coach. For a coach there is the opportunity to learn or develop new skills such as communication and leadership, to improve one's self-confidence, meet new people and challenge oneself in a competitive environment. And it is hard to measure the satisfaction to be derived from seeing young people develop as well-rounded human beings.

ACKNOWLEDGEMENTS

The authors would like to thank Emily Sweet, Charlotte Atyeo and Nick Humphrey at Bloomsbury; Rafique Ossman and others for their participation in the photo shoots; everyone involved with Ealing Cricket Club for their help with hosting the photo shoots; Grant Pritchard and Graham Morris for their excellent photographs; Greg Stevenson for producing the diagrams of the various drills.

Rob Maier would like to thank the many people who have assisted his coaching career and shared or inspired ideas over the years. Specifically, Steve Ayres, of Chesham CC and formerly Buckinghamshire's cricket development officer; Chris Peploe and Leigh Parry, Rob's fellow head coaches at PPM Cricket Coaching; Toby Radford, former Middlesex head coach and current West Indies assistant coach; Graeme West, formerly Middlesex CCC academy director and current head of West Indies high-performance centre in Barbados; Rory Coutts, Middlesex's cricket development officer; Neil Rider, Berkshire's cricket development officer; Andy Wagner of Middlesex CCC and Radley College; Peter Wellings; Josh Knappett of Middlesex CCC and Alan Coleman, assistant academy director at Middlesex.

ABOUT THE AUTHORS

Rob Maier grew up in Durban, South Africa, and shared the new ball with Shaun Pollock for South Africa Schools. He moved to the UK in 1997 and is an ECB-qualified Level 3 coach. He has coached Middlesex CCC age-group sides (U13 to U16) since 2004 and has been a coach at Harrow School since 2009. He has been a professional and director of coaching at Chesham CC in Buckinghamshire. He has coached youngsters of all ages and abilities.

John Stern was editor of the *Wisden Cricketer* magazine from its launch in 2003 to 2011. He writes on cricket for a number of national and international publications, including *The Times*, *All Out Cricket* magazine and *Wisden Cricketers' Almanack*. As an opening batsman for Wendover CC in Buckinghamshire, he had his best ever season after a winter of one-to-one sessions with Rob Maier.